JERUSALEM FOOD

JERUSALEM FOOD

Bold Flavors from the Middle East and Beyond

NIDAL KERSH

STERLING EPICURE
New York

CONTENTS

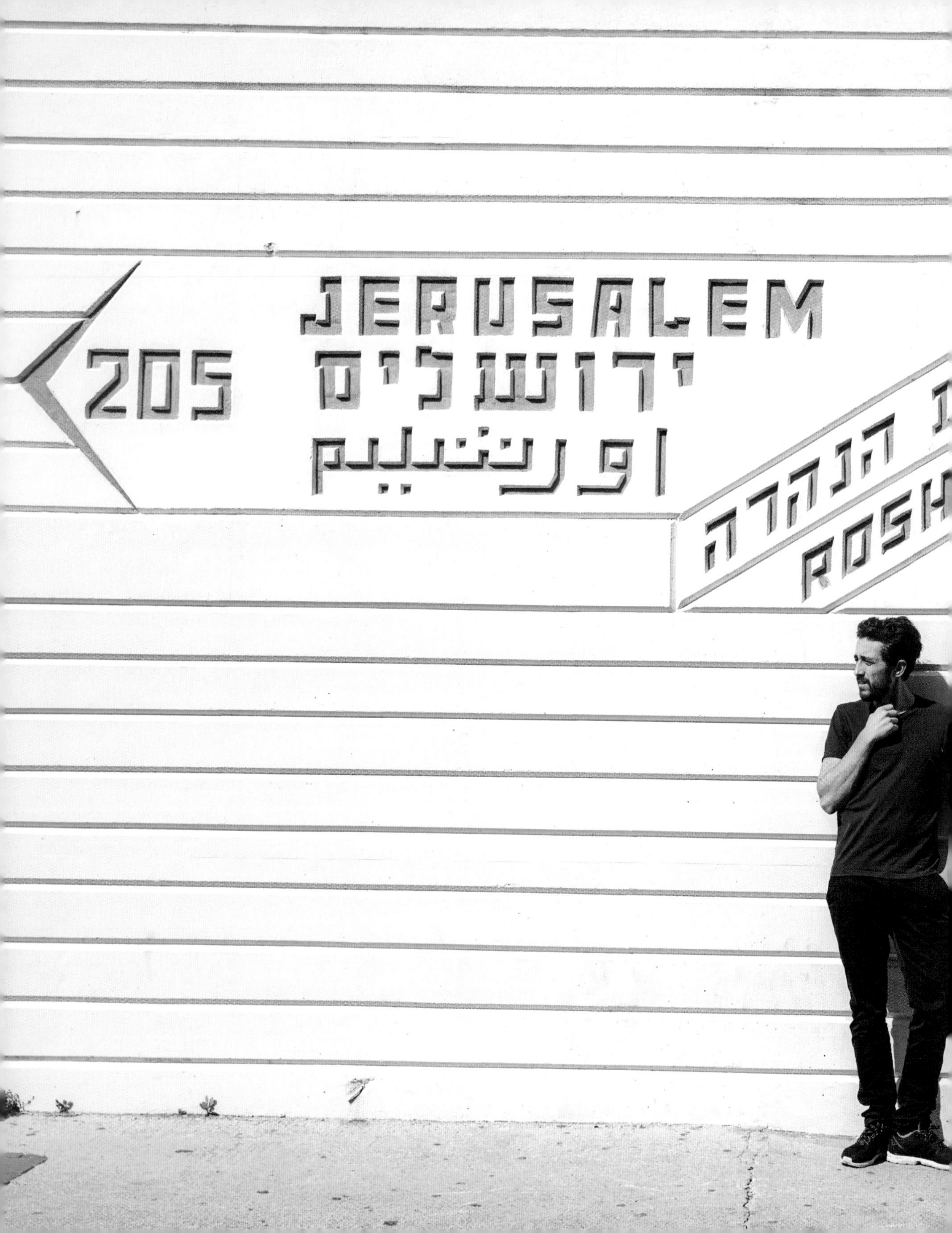
JERUSALEM
205
ירושלים
اورشليم

I'm standing in front of the Lebanese border on the Israeli side, in a place called Rosh Hanikra, or Ras il Naqoura in Arabic. The sign shows how far it is to Beirut and Jerusalem from where I stand. The names Beirut and Jerusalem are translated into English, Hebrew, and Arabie, but the Arabic name Al-Quds is instead translated as the Hebrew name, Urshalim.

{ Beyond Jerusalem }

Shakshuka is the name of a dish that originally comes from North Africa. It is a stew that consists of tomato sauce, chili, coriander, and eggs. *Shakshuka* also means *to mix* or *shake up*, and in many ways it exemplifies the melting pot of food—and culture—that has emerged in Jerusalem. Sometimes it's cooked well and sometimes, to put it mildly, it all boils over. . . . And sometimes the eggs become too hard-boiled.

Jerusalem is a center for three world religions: Judaism, Christianity, and Islam. It's a meeting place for people from all over the world, and its kitchens reflect that diversity. Jerusalem is also a place where people may live side by side and yet never really meet. It is precisely because the city is so diverse that simple dishes, like hummus or falafel, have taken on more importance than the food itself and become powerful expressions of identity and belonging.

Much of what is eaten in Jerusalem, and around Palestine and Israel, is not, in some ways, unique to the Middle East. However, conflicts between Palestinians and Israelis have given certain dishes intense meaning, which can trigger strong feelings. Some dishes are loaded with politics and symbolism. For the Palestinians, food has become one of the last markers of their identity.

My interest in cooking started when I moved away from home. Before that, food, for me, was all about the atmosphere that cooking created. I always helped in the kitchen, although only with dishwashing. I don't think I chopped an onion until I moved away from home, but all that time in the kitchen as a dishwasher nevertheless had an effect on me. I must have subconsciously noticed how my dad often used three frying pans for each dish he made, and how he moved like a storm

You don't need a cutting board to slice onions—a knife and your own hands will do.

Sweden, where I born and raised, and in Palestine, when we visited our relatives on summer holidays. There were classic dishes like mana'ish, shawarma, baba ganouj, and baklava, as well as olives and Greek yogurt, with lots of za'atar and olive oil, freshly baked pita bread, and watermelon. Food was always the biggest topic of conversation, from the moment we woke up in the morning until it was time to sleep in the evening.

through the kitchen, creating chaos, as he prepared dish after dish. My friends always said that our home smelled of cooking food, which is probably true. If there was anything we had at home, it was food. My brothers and I never needed to ask if friends were allowed to come over and eat. There was always enough food for guests.

Many of the recipes in this book are for dishes we used to eat at home in

Fresh, green sweet almonds, delicious with a little salt.

{ A Family History }

When the Arab-Israeli War broke out in the spring of 1948, my grandfather was hunting just outside of Mazra'a, his hometown. He had borrowed a rifle and targeted a bird but never got a chance to fire a shot, because a man named General McNeill, whom everyone in Mazra'a called Il Inglizi ("the Englishman"), happened to see him. McNeill gave my grandfather a reprimand that would save his life and his village: "Mahmoud! Are you out of your mind? They're going to bomb Smiriyeh! Don't you understand what would happen if they hear a shot from here? Go home and stay there until it's all over." My grandfather went home. He had no idea that the war had broken out, but it had. And nothing would ever be the same. Everyone sat at home and could hear the fighting only a few kilometers away. They were afraid of what would happen, but there was nothing else to do other than to wait. Sure enough, Smiriyeh, the neighboring village, was bombarded later that day and leveled to the ground.

All the villages and cities around Mazra'a suffered from the war. My grandfather didn't know exactly how old he was when the war broke out, but he was probably eighteen. From early on, he had worked for General McNeill, who, with his wife, lived in the oldest house in Mazra'a—and it was his presence that saved the village. In 1948, he and his wife did not follow his fellow British countrymen out of the country, which was until then called Mandatory Palestine. They stayed in Mazra'a. But, after 1948, Palestine no longer existed. The new state was called Israel, and Mazra'a became a refugee camp for

Palestinians who fled from the nearby villages of Galilee.

When my grandfather was born, only a few families lived in Mazra'a, but soon many more were sharing space in the village. For over a decade, my grandfather lived under Israeli military law and had to apply for permission to leave the village. He married a nice girl from Akko, my grandmother, and for her, life in the village came as a bit of a shock. She had to exchange an indoor toilet and servants for an outhouse and daily life with the entire family.

One day my grandfather's father came to the house to speak with him. His brother was going to marry and had nowhere to live. My grandfather, who was the oldest son in the family and actually had the right to live in the house, interpreted his father's words to mean that he had been asked to move. After that conversation, my grandfather discussed the matter with his friend Fattin, who owned some land at the edge of the village. Fattin gave him permission to live there. My grandfather immediately got on his bicycle and rode over to the land, which was pure wilderness at the time, but he found some old oil barrels, took them apart, and built a small hut. He then fetched my grandmother and my two uncles, and they moved into their new home. After they arrived, my

From Ras al-Naqoura you have a fantastic view of the Galilean coastline and Mediterranean Sea.

The horses grazing in the meadow are Arabian full bloods. In the background you can see the villages of Abu Snan and Kafr Yasif.

grandmother asked my grandfather what they would eat and if they could go back to their old home to get some flour and bulgur, so they would have something to eat that night. My grandfather got on his bike, but because of his pride, he could not go back to his old house to pick up food. Instead, he found an orange tree and filled a basket with the fruit and brought it back to his new home.

My dad grew up in that tiny hut. He was born in 1958 and was the fourth of eight children. The hut rusted at regular intervals, so my grandfather would pull apart new oil barrels to repair it. One day, an Israeli official came to Mazra'a and explained to Fattin that the land he owned was no longer his and now belonged to the state. Fattin went out of his mind that day, and the last time anyone saw him, he was on his way out of the village, talking to himself, never to return. My grandfather was allowed to rent what had been Fattin's land from the state, but there were many in Mazra'a who lost their land, and most of the village's arable land was given to the kibbutzim* to use.

A man whom the villagers called Abu Josef worked at a kibbutz nearby.

What his real name was, my grandfather didn't remember, but Abu Josef always gave the villagers access to the kibbutz's field after the harvest, when there was a little wheat left that the tractor had missed. However, you risked a serious beating if you went into the fields without Abu Josef's permission.

In my grandfather's day Mazra'a was green and wild and the kids played outdoors. In the winter, the old aqueduct filled with water and the children in the village used it as a slide. The winter was also a time for oranges, which the family ate, as well as bulgur, lentils, beans, and bread that my grandmother baked in a clay oven. They had some goats that gave milk and some hens for eggs and meat.

My grandfather initially worked as a day laborer at different kibbutzim. After a few years, he got a job at "il baladye" (district administration) in Naharya. When it was time for a meal, there was always more bread than filling and my grandfather always ate the least of all, making sure everyone else was full. His approach to food followed him throughout his life. He always ate moderately, no matter how much food was on the table. He quoted the Prophet as

* Communal farms or settlements

saying that one should fill the stomach with one-third food, one-third water, and one-third air.

In the spring, my grandfather and grandmother used to take the whole family to the mountains to pick za'atar. They would cut off the leaves without removing the roots, so that they could return in the autumn to harvest the new growth. In the summer, they visited the ruins of old villages and picked prickly pears. All Palestinian villages had cacti, too, and although the houses might disappear, the cacti would always return. My grandfather and all of my uncles participated in the cactus-picking and came home with full buckets.

Around Mazra'a, houses were being built for the influx of new Israelis, who came from all corners of the world. They needed labor, and the Palestinians were ready to help build new homes on the land where, only a few years earlier, there had been Palestinian villages. By the end of the 1970s, the family's economic situation improved to the extent that they could afford to build a real house, which they did, with the expert help of my oldest uncle Husni, who eventually became a construction engineer.

The house was finished sometime in the mid-1980s. In Arab villages in Israel, there was no city planning. Many built their houses illegally, because the land was officially classified as cultivation land; but the need to build was too great, and the state didn't help. If you hurried and just built on the land, the authorities would sometimes let the matter go. You paid a fine, but at least you could keep your house. My grandmother and grandfather lived on the bottom floor, and there were four additional apartments for my uncles, as well as one for my dad, but at the time he wasn't particularly interested in a life in the village. Early on, he realized that he wouldn't stay, so he dropped out of high school and found work at a hotel in the city of Naharya, which was a mile away from Mazra'a and had been founded by German-Jewish immigrants in the late-nineteenth century. The difference between Mazra'a and Naharya was like night and day. There was no comparison between the shanties in Mazra'a and the fine villas along the coast or the cafés, restaurants, and discos in Naharya. For Mazra's inhabitants, Naharya was far away (like a different world). You visited the city if you had to go to the bank or receive your salary or visit the hospital. Otherwise,

there was no reason to be in Naharya. It was like an invisible barrier between the Israelis and Arabs. My dad, however, unknowingly broke the barrier. He wanted to be where the Israelis were, in the sense that he didn't want to accept that some areas, places, and even dreams were reserved for Israelis but not for him. He worked his way up in the restaurant business by working in Nahariya's most popular hotels. At that time northern Israel was very popular among European tourists, who would spend time there working in kibbutzim. This gave my father opportunities to meet some of them and inspired him to travel and see Europe.

Soon, the journeys to Europe began. My father traveled to Germany, the Netherlands, Denmark, and finally Sweden. In Sweden he met my mom, who had just moved there from Finland. She worked in a Jewish retirement home as a cook and lived in the servant's quarters at Katarina Bangata in Södermalm in Stockholm. They met at a pizzeria, fell in love, had three children, became unhappy and divorced, and became happy again. And so that's the way it has been.

My uncle Samir is a car mechanic and has his own workshop. He has a fondness for old cars, and when we were young he had a Volvo Amazon, which he cared for meticulously. While working on this book, we wanted to photograph really old olive trees, and Samir had just the right vehicle for the excursion: an old Mercedes from the 1950s, which he had completely restored. Behind the sign on the left you can see the destination of our trip—an olive tree that is close to one thousand years old.

Jumping from this sea wall is a rite of passage for all of Akko's residents. As a six-year-old, my little brother Samir set a new standard when he jumped from the forty-nine-foot-high (fifteen-meter) wall right down into the ocean.

{ Akko }

The year is 1191. The crusaders, led by Richard the Lionheart, have conquered Akko after a long siege. Sultan Saladin, who just a few years before had managed to drive the crusaders from Palestine, could only watch helplessly. His reinforcements never arrived, and ultimately Akko had little desire to continue resisting a siege that had lasted for several months. Akko would be the final outpost of the Holy Kingdom of Jerusalem. The crusaders never succeeded in conquering Jerusalem again, but they remained in Akko until 1291. A city with so much history also remembers events as if they'd happened yesterday. To this day, people still talk about how, after the siege, Richard the Lionheart took all three thousand hostages up to the top of Akko's wall and beheaded them in front of Saladin. Richard wanted to go on to lay siege to Jerusalem, and the hostages would only cost him food and time.

Traces of the crusaders still exist in Akko, in the names of neighborhoods, like *suq il franj* (Frenchmen's square) and *il bizani* (Pisa), and in buildings, such as

Akko, the city where my father's family came from, is mentioned in the Old Testament and is one of the world's oldest cities. My father's mother was born in Akko and lived there until she married my grandfather and moved to Mazra'a. These pictures were taken in the oldest part of Akko.

the citadel and the underground tunnels that allowed soldiers to move quickly to different parts of the city under attack.

Akko has been around for at least five thousand years, although the exact location has changed slightly over the millennia. Modern Akko gained its current form after the Ottomans conquered the city in 1517. Akko's most famous buildings were constructed by Ahmad Pasha, also known as Al-Jazzar, which means "the butcher" in Arabic. As a young man, Ahmad (whose title—Pasha—was equivalent to an English viscount) earned this nickname after taking revenge on a Bedouin tribe for killing one of his friends. He originally came from Bosnia, but through a long and not completely straight-and-narrow career, he eventually became governor of Akko in 1776.

Al-Jazzar is described as having been tough but also fair. His biggest achievement was defending Akko from Napoleon in 1799, which interrupted his conquest of Palestine. To this day Al-Jazzar is famous for this defeat: "Not even Napoleon managed to cross Akko's walls!" It is said that when Napoleon gave up after a siege lasting sixty-three days, he threw his hat over the wall so that at least something of him would find its way into Akko.

Al-Jazzar left behind an Akko that was richer than when he arrived. He built an aqueduct that secured a fresh water supply from Al-Kabri in northern Galilee, reinforced the walls that protected the city, and built a great mosque in which he was eventually buried. Al-Jazzar also built markets in the city, where travelers could stay a few days and exchange goods. This was also a way for Al-Jazzar to ensure tax revenue. He also built a big *hamam* (Turkish bath) that was completed in 1781. My grandmother used to go to that hamam until the war of 1948, when it was closed.

In the mid-1850s, Palestinian citrus growers in the city of Jaffa cultivated an orange that was sweet and almost seedless. The orange's thick, easy-to-peel rind was well-suited for long journeys. It would be called the Jaffa orange and became an enormously successful export worldwide.

In addition to its history, Akko is also an interesting place for food! It is said that Akko's inhabitants invented hummus during the crusaders' long siege. Today there are a dozen hummus restaurants, many of which are considered to be among the best in the country. Fish and shellfish, as well as organ meats, are an important part of the food culture in Akko, and they continue to be popular.

Akko has a special place in my life. During a period in high school, my whole family moved from Stockholm to Akko, where my dad opened a restaurant. It was a stone's throw from the sea, and my brothers and I used to spend our days swimming from the rocks and jumping from Akko's high walls. I never became a good fisherman, but my brothers did. We went to a Catholic school called Terra Santa. The principal of the school was a priest from Italy. (My dad had also attended Terra Santa, and the school is still considered the best in the area.) The discipline was strict, but you got used to it. There was a school uniform but no school lunch. You brought your own food or bought it at the market.

What I remember most about Akko are all the intense scents—sometimes fragrant and sometimes not-so fragrant—of everything from spices to fish guts, the cool alleys, and the sea. But I also remember the sounds—the loud discussions, the laughter, and the calls to prayer.

During the 1990s, after the fall of the Soviet Union, nearly nine hundred thousand Russian speakers from different parts of the former Soviet Union emigrated to Israel. Therefore, it's not unusual to see signs like this one, with prices in Hebrew, Arabic, and Russian.

Abu George is a famous hummus restaurant in historic Akko. The restaurant is located right next to the Al-Jazzar mosque.

{ It's Complicated }

My first memories of Palestine go back to when I was six years old. We never said "Israel," and with the limited knowledge I had, I thought the airport was Israel, mostly because of the long checkpoints and because I didn't understand the language. I thought our city of Mazra'a was Palestine, because they spoke Arabic there.

In December 2016, the UN Security Council voted for a resolution condemning Israeli settlements in Palestinian territory that had been occupied since 1967. The Security Council reaffirmed that the settlements had no legal validity and were an obstacle to peace and the future of two states living peacefully, side by side, within internationally recognized borders. Israel responded by granting building permits for three thousand new residential homes. Even today, settlements are increasing. The areas and roads that connect the settlements often cut through arable land and olive groves. It's frequently impossible to work the fields, and sometimes the Palestinians

are allowed to manage their crops only once a year.

Both the Palestinians living in Israel as Israeli citizens and the Palestinians living under occupation in the West Bank and Gaza have, at best, a complicated relationship with Israel. Palestinians often live under oppression, and even though they actually live in the same country with Israelis, and enjoy many of the same types of food, they are divided and segregated. Palestinians and Israelis go to different schools, rarely live in the same areas, and, to some extent, don't speak each other's languages. Palestinians in Israel understand and speak Hebrew, but it is unusual for Israelis to understand Arabic. Palestinians live stateless in occupied areas in which their basic existence is subordinate under Israeli military power.

To understand why it's complicated to talk about food in Israel and Palestine, one must understand its history and what the food symbolizes for the different people living there. My

family lives in the place where they have always lived, but the Israeli identity into which we've been assimilated is not quite as easy to relate to. We do not just see ourselves as another group of Palestinians because we don't live in the occupied areas.

Food is not just food in Israel and Palestine. Hummus is not just a dish; it's a symbol. For the Palestinians it is a symbol that says we ate hummus before you and we are still eating hummus. Meanwhile, the Israelis search for biblical evidence that hummus was eaten during King David's time, to prove that the Israelis did not take hummus from the Palestinians.

Neither historic Palestine nor modern Israel has ever been ethnically or religiously homogeneous, and as long as the conflict continues to focus on who owns the country instead of coming to the conclusion that everyone belongs there, we will never reach a peaceful solution. It's possible to live together, but for it to work it's necessary to have equal rights.

Elet (chicory)

Khobezi (mallow)

Green almonds

Shomar (wild dill)

Hommeda (wild greens)

{ Food Culture and Memories }

I remember that my grandmother always used to sit on the porch in Mazra'a. She usually kept an eye on the street, where we kids used to play. One of her first questions after saying "good morning" was always what we wanted to eat for lunch or for dinner and, depending on the answer, she would then ask my grandfather to go shopping for what was needed. My grandfather had a bicycle that looked like it went all the way back to the British occupation, and he rode it everywhere. He never got his driver's license and cycled everywhere instead. Once the police stopped him and said he was cycling too fast on the highway.

Sometimes we got to go with him when we said we wanted to eat *molokhia* (also known as Jute mallow, the leaves and young fruits are used as a vegetable). A little ways outside the village, he had a small plot where he grew okra, molokhia, spinach, squash, and a lot of other things. If there was not enough homegrown produce for whatever dish my grandmother planned to make, he

rode his bike to Akko and bought some at the market.

When it was time to eat, my grandmother called out loudly so that everyone in the house could hear. All the cousins would come down, along with the uncles who were at home and their wives. If we were going on a trip, my grandmother filled pita bread with fried eggs for us or prepared mana'ish (an olive oil–rich flatbread topped with za'atar), packed in plastic bags together with some small cucumbers and fruit if we were lucky.

My grandfather liked everything my grandmother made with one exception: anything with coriander. He detested it so much, he didn't even want it in the house. On the other hand, he liked strong food, and at lunch he would always eat chili peppers that my grandmother roasted in the oven with a little olive oil. My brothers, cousins, and I used to dare one another to taste them. Sometimes we'd take a bite and then run around the yard like hens, shouting for water.

There is a long tradition in Palestine of picking wild herbs and plants. Here, my aunt Husnye shows me which ones to pick.

In the 1990s, it was still common for Palestinian salespeople from the West Bank and Gaza to pass by the village in pickup trucks filled with goods. My grandmother was a very good negotiator, and one day she happened to buy a load of watermelons. The price she offered was so low that, at first, the seller refused. Then she said that if she got that price, she'd buy all the melons in the truck. The seller saw his chance to go home a little earlier and accepted. We ate a lot of watermelon that summer.

Every weekend, my uncle Mustafa used to take us to a park called Al-Zeeb. Until the 1948 war, the park was in a Palestinian city by the sea, but today there are only ruins. One house remains, though—the house where my grandmother's sister lived, before she fled. As a child, we never thought about that. It was the sea that grabbed all our attention. We bathed and learned how to catch fish by using a large can with bread on the bottom and then waiting for the fish to swim in. We usually stayed on the beach all day until the sun went down. When it was time for dinner, my uncle grilled for us. We always brought in coolers fully loaded with meat, vegetables, and side dishes.

Many of my memories are about food— the social glue that held our family together. My grandmother continued to cook for the whole family, although it wasn't necessary. I don't know if she did it consciously or unconsciously, but she cooked food for all her children, grandchildren, and even her great-grandchildren for as long as she could. It was an expression of generosity, in which a guest could never leave her home without receiving something to eat.

In our family, you eat everything with bread and no meal is complete without it. My grandmother and grandfather always showed great reverence for bread and it was never thrown away. If it became too dry, my grandfather gave it to the birds. If you dropped bread on the floor, you picked it up, brushed it off, and touched the bread to your forehead as an act of asking God's forgiveness for being careless with something as important as bread. The classic Arab way to eat is to cook a bowl of food and then eat from the bowl using bread. Depending on how many are going to eat from the common dish, you need to imagine invisible pieces of torn bread, evenly distributed among those who are eating. It's always courteous to ask others to help themselves first. Today, we might set a fancy

Sinarye, the plant above, is eaten in spring, when the stalk is still soft. When my uncles were young and out and about, they ate the super-moist, cucumber-like stalks if they were thirsty.

table with plates and cutlery, but we still use bread to eat from the common bowl. My uncle usually looks surprised when I eat chicken with cutlery and blurts out, "Why are you eating like that? It doesn't taste as good!"

Our food culture is characterized by great generosity and hospitality. As a guest, you're always invited to share the meal. If you're a guest, then you're the center of attention, and the host family will make sure you leave the table full and satisfied. Traditions, such as this one, derive from Bedouin customs, and there is a saying that even a stranger is a guest if a stranger happens to come to your home.

Ingredients in Palestinian dishes are very similar to those that can be found all around the Mediterranean. There are lots of vegetables, beans, lentils, and wheat in various forms. The closer you live to the coast, the more fish is eaten. The meats one traditionally eats are chicken and lamb, which is used sparingly for flavor, except during big feasts when a lamb is slaughtered and cooked whole.

In Palestine, coffee is the preferred warm beverage, and one drinks it throughout the day. It is usually served sweet and seasoned with cardamom. Coffee is served in small cups called *finjan,* and it's common for a guest to receive a cup of coffee as a welcoming gesture, as well as a way of saying goodbye. At funerals and weddings you are served a special coffee from Yemen called *qahwa sada*, which translates to something along the lines of "simple coffee," in the sense that it's not been sweetened. It is very strong coffee that has simmered for several hours.

There are several major markets throughout the country. Under Ottoman rule, the markets were an important source of income for the cities, which were visited by farmers and merchants, from near and far, and were where they paid a tax to sell their goods.

The olive tree below is over seven hundred years old and still provides plenty of olives every year. If you take care of olive trees, like this one, they can grow even older.

The olive oil and olives, shown above, came from this olive grove. The family that owns the trees allowed us to photograph them and generously gave us the olives and oil as a gift.

Spices like cumin, cloves, ginger, and paprika are important foundations for building flavor. These spices are often mixed together and simply called *baharat*, which means "spices." There are different spice mixtures for fish and meat, and when you go to the souk (the market), you buy your favorites from the spice merchant who makes the best combinations.

BAHARAT All-Purpose

» **Makes about ⅔ cup (2 dl)**

1 tablespoon ground black pepper

3 tablespoons ground coriander

1 tablespoon ground cinnamon

2 teaspoons ground cloves

3 tablespoons ground cumin

2 teaspoons ground cardamom

2 teaspoons ground nutmeg

4 tablespoons paprika

1 tablespoon ground ginger

1 teaspoon ground allspice

- In a small bowl, mix together all of the ingredients until they are well combined. Store the spice mixture in a glass jar with a lid.

BAHARAT for Chicken & Meat

» **Makes about 1 cup (2½ dl)**

1 tablespoon ground black pepper

3 tablespoons ground coriander

1 tablespoon ground cinnamon

2 teaspoons ground cloves

3 tablespoons ground cumin

2 teaspoons ground cardamom

2 teaspoons ground nutmeg

4 tablespoons paprika

1 tablespoon ground ginger

1 teaspoon ground allspice

1 tablespoon ground fenugreek

1 tablespoon ground turmeric

1 tablespoon dried garlic

- In a small bowl, mix together all of the ingredients until they are well combined. Store the spice mixture in a glass jar with a lid.

SUMAC

Sumac is a berry that grows all over the Mediterranean. In the Middle East, it is used as a spice. It has an acidic taste and plays an important role in flavoring a variety of dishes, including fattoush (see recipe on page 80) and musakhan (see recipe on page 122).

ZA'ATAR

Za'atar refers to both a spice mixture and the different varieties of oregano and thyme. The best variety is Syrian oregano, *Origanum syriacum*, which is nearly impossible to find unless you live in a Mediterranean country and can walk up into the mountains to pick your own. Za'atar, the mixture, combines oregano, thyme, sumac, roasted sesame seeds, and a little salt. It is also an important feature of Palestinian food culture.

» **Makes about 1¾ cup (4 dl)**

7 tablespoons (1 dl) dried oregano

7 tablespoons (1 dl) ground sumac

7 tablespoons (1 dl) roasted sesame seeds

1 tablespoon salt

• In a small bowl, stir together all of the ingredients until they are well combined. Store the spice mixture in a jar with a lid. You can use za'atar to flavor just about anything: Stir it into yogurt, use it to season pasta sauce, or sprinkle it over mana'ish (see recipes on pages 37–42).

BREAD

PITA BREAD [*ikmaj*]

This is the bread that one eats most often. In Arabic it's called *ikmaj*, and in Hebrew it is called *pita*, from the Greek name for bread. While it's baking, the bread rises and puffs up, and when it's sliced, you can use it as a handy pocket to fill with falafel or anything else you might enjoy.

» **Makes 10–12 pitas**

1 ounce (25 g) fresh yeast

2 teaspoons salt

1¾ cups (4 dl) cold water

3¾–4¼ cups (9–10 dl) flour

1. In a large bowl, stir the yeast and salt together. Add the water until the mixture is well combined. Mix in almost all of the flour and work the dough until the texture is smooth. The dough should be a bit sticky, but it should hold together. Cover the bowl with plastic wrap and place it in the refrigerator overnight.

2. When you're ready to bake the pita, preheat the oven to 475°F (250°C). Remove the dough from the fridge. Sprinkle flour on a dry surface to prevent sticking and knead the dough until it is smooth. Divide the dough into 10–12 3½-ounce (100-g) pieces and shape them into small buns. Place them on a dry surface and cover them with a clean dishtowel. Let the dough rest and rise for about 30 minutes. Place a pizza stone or baking sheet in the oven while the dough rises.

3. Once the dough has risen, roll the buns out into rounds, each about 6 inches (15 cm) in diameter. Remove the pizza stone from the oven and lightly flour it, working quickly. Place the rounds on the stone and put it in the oven to bake. Bake the bread for 3–5 minutes or until it puffs up and becomes golden brown. Remove the bread from the oven and let it cool before serving.

Tip!

* Place leftover pitas in a sealable storage bag and freeze them for later use.

* Put aside a third of the dough to make za'atar sticks (see recipe on page 35).

ZA'ATAR STICKS

Use a portion of the dough from the pita bread recipe on page 33 to make these spicy bread sticks. Enjoy them with your favorite dips.

» **Makes 20 sticks**

⅓ **of the dough from the pita bread recipe, see page 33**

¼ **cup (½ dl) za'atar, see recipe on page 28**

1. Preheat the oven to 425°F (220°C). Prepare the dough for pita bread (see recipe, page 33). When you mix in the flour, add the za'atar.

2. Divide the dough and roll it out into thick, 4-inch-long (1 dm) sticks. Place the dough on a dry surface and cover it with a clean dishtowel. Allow the dough to rest and rise for 30 minutes.

3. Once the dough has risen, transfer it to a baking sheet. Bake the za'atar sticks in the oven for 5–10 minutes. When they're done, remove the bread sticks from the oven and let them cool before serving.

My aunt Husnye makes
the best mana'ish.

Mana'ish

MANA'ISH (Arabic pizza)

Mana'ish Dough

Mana'ish is the Middle East's answer to pizza. What really makes it special are toppings like za'atar with olive oil, onions roasted with sumac and paprika, or labneh. One of my favorite ways to eat freshly baked mana'ish is for breakfast, alongside a cup of green tea with fresh mint and sugar. When mana'ish glistens with olive oil, it's difficult to resist, even if it's too hot to eat.

» **Makes 10–15 pizzas**

1 batch of pita bread, see recipe page 33

Toppings, see suggestions on pages 40–42

1. Prepare the dough according to the recipe for pita bread. Divide the dough and roll out into rounds, each about 6 inches (15 cm) in diameter. Place the rounds on a dry surface and cover them with a baking towel to rest and rise for about 30 minutes. After 30 minutes, lightly press down on the dough to prevent it from rising when baking.

2. While the dough is resting, preheat the oven to 475°F (250°C). If your oven doesn't get that hot, keep the temperature as high as possible.

3. Before baking, top each round of dough with one or more toppings (see suggestions on pages 40–42) or make your own. Bake the bread for about 5 minutes.

LAHM BI AJIN

» **Makes 4 pizzas**

1 large yellow onion

4 garlic cloves

3 tomatoes

1 fresh chili pepper, any
  kind

olive oil for frying

7 ounces (200 g) ground
  lamb or beef

1 teaspoon baharat for
  chicken and meat,
  see recipe on page 26

salt

freshly ground black pepper

1. Prepare the dough for the pizza crust (see recipe on page 39).

2. Preheat the oven to 475°F (250°C).

3. As the dough rises, peel and chop the onion and garlic. Dice the tomatoes and chop the chili pepper.

4. In a frying pan, heat the oil. Add the onions and garlic and sauté until translucent. Add the meat and the baharat and cook until the meat is browned. Once the meat is cooked, add the tomatoes and chili pepper and let the mixture simmer until all the liquid has boiled off. Season it with salt and pepper and set it aside.

5. When the pizza dough is ready, top it with the meat mixture and bake it for about 5 minutes, preferably on a pizza stone or hot pan, until it becomes golden brown.

MANA'ISH WITH LABNEH

» **Makes 6–8 pizzas**

1 quart (1 l) plain yogurt

olive oil for serving

1. To make the labneh, place the yogurt in a cheesecloth or coffee filter over a bowl. Place the bowl in the refrigerator and let the yogurt drain for at least 8 hours, until it is thick and creamy.

2. Preheat the oven to 475°F (250°C).

3. When the labneh is ready, make the dough for the pizza crust (see recipe on page 39). Spread the labneh over the top of the dough and bake for about 5 minutes. Remove the pizza from the oven and drizzle it with olive oil before serving.

MANA'ISH IB BASAL [with Onion]

» **Makes 6–7 pizzas**

3 yellow onions

**½ cup (1 dl) olive oil +
    extra for frying**

salt

**2 tablespoons bell pepper
    or tomato paste**

**a pinch of baharat, see
    recipe on page 26**

optional: **a little harissa or
    hot sauce**

1. Prepare the dough for the pizza crust (see recipe on page 39).

2. Preheat the oven to 475°F (250°C). Peel and dice the onions. In a saucepan over low heat, add a little oil. When the oil is hot, add the onions and season with a pinch of salt, which will help the onions sweat and cook faster as you fry them. Stir the onions gently until they become translucent.

3. Remove the saucepan from the heat. Combine the cooked onions with the ½ cup oil, bell pepper paste or tomato paste, baharat, and harissa, if desired. Stir to combine. The mixture should resemble pesto.

4. Spread the mixture over the top of the dough and place it on a prepared pizza stone or hot pan. Bake the pizza for about 5 minutes, serve.

Onion mixture for *mana'ish ib basal*

MANA'ISH IB ZA'ATAR (with Za'atar)

» **Makes 6 pizzas**

½ cup (1 dl) za'atar, see
   recipe on page 29

3 tablespoons (½ dl)
   olive oil

3 medium tomatoes

1 bunch mint

1 lemon, sliced in half

1. Preheat the oven to 475°F (250°C). Prepare the
   dough for the pizza crust (see recipe on page 39).
   In a bowl, combine the za'atar and oil, stirring
   together until it resembles pesto. Spread the
   za'atar mixture onto the rolled-out dough.

2. Bake the dough on a pizza stone or hot pan for
   about 5 minutes.

3. While the dough is baking, roughly chop the
   tomatoes and separate the mint leaves.

4. Remove the bread from the oven and squeeze a
   lemon half over it. Top the hot bread with the
   tomatoes and mint. Enjoy, preferably with a cup
   of mint tea (see recipe on page 168).

Mana'ish with onion
[page 41]

Mana'ish with za'atar
[page 42]

JERUSALEM BREAD

In Arabic, this bread is called *ka'ak*, a word that is also used for sweet bread or cakes. Similar breads are made everywhere in the Middle East, but this particular bread, a specialty of the city, is called *ka'ak il quds*, or Jerusalem bread. It comes in various shapes, and of course it tastes better in Jerusalem than anywhere else.

» Makes 6–8 loaves

1 ounce (25 g) fresh yeast

3 cups (7 dl) lukewarm water

5 teaspoons granulated sugar

6–7 cups (14–16.5 dl) flour

3 teaspoons salt

6 tablespoons neutral oil, such as sunflower oil or peanut oil

1¼ cups (3 dl) white sesame seeds

1. In a bowl, combine the yeast, lukewarm water, and sugar. Let the mixture sit for 10 minutes to activate the yeast.

2. In a separate bowl, mix the flour and salt until well combined. Add the yeast mixture and oil to the bowl and knead the dough until it is smooth. Cover the bowl with a towel and allow the dough to rest and rise for 45 minutes.

3. After 45 minutes, divide the dough into smaller balls and place them on a clean, flour-dusted surface. Leave some space around each of the balls so that they will have room to rise. Loosely cover the dough with plastic wrap and let it rise again for at least 45 minutes.

4. Preheat the oven to 425°F (220°C).

5. Line 2 baking pans with parchment paper. Once the dough has risen again, form each dough ball into a ring.

6. Pour the sesame seeds into a shallow dish. Dip the dough rings into the sesame seeds (or sprinkle them over the dough, if you prefer)—there can't be too many sesame seeds—and place them on the prepared pan. Let the dough rings rest for another 15 minutes.

7. Place the baking pans in the oven and bake the dough for 15–25 minutes, rotating the pans halfway through. Keep an eye on the bread throughout the baking time. It should be golden brown, not burned. When the bread is done, remove it from the oven. You can serve it just as it is or with olive oil and za'atar.

SAUCES AND DIPS

TAHINI SAUCE

Tahini sauce pairs well with just about everything. It is also rich in protein, calcium, fiber, and healthy fats. Some enjoy tahini with sesame pasta; try it in some of your favorite dishes and see if you like it. For a great variation, add garlic and dill or any other herbs you may have on hand to the mix.

» **Makes about 2 cups [5 dl]**

2 garlic cloves

⅔ cup (2 dl) tahini

½ cup (1 dl) freshly
　squeezed lemon juice

1¼ cups (3 dl) water

1 teaspoon salt

• Peel the garlic cloves. Combine all the ingredients in a bowl. Using an immersion blender or hand mixer, blend the sauce until it is completely smooth.

TARATOUR

Taratour is a variation of tahini sauce that is made with parsley, which gives the sauce a beautiful light green color. It pairs particularly well with fish. For additional flavor, you can add chopped tomatoes and onions to the mix.

» **Makes about 2 cups [5 dl]**

2 garlic cloves

⅔ cup (2 dl) tahini

juice of 1 lemon

⅔ cup (2 dl) water

1 bunch parsley

1 teaspoon salt

• Peel the garlic cloves. Combine all the ingredients in a bowl and blend them with a hand mixer until the sauce is completely smooth.

HARISSA

Middle Eastern people use harrisa the same way Americans use ketchup. The difference between the two condiments? Harissa is much hotter.

» Makes about 1 cup [2–3 dl]

1 teaspoon caraway seeds

1 teaspoon cumin seeds

1 teaspoon coriander seeds

3½ ounces (100 g) mixed dried and fresh chilis, any kind

2 garlic cloves

1 teaspoon salt

½ cup (1 dl) neutral oil, such as sunflower oil or peanut oil

¼–½ cup (½–1 dl) water

1. Preheat the oven to 400°F (200°C). In a frying pan, toast the caraway, cumin, and coriander seeds. Once toasted, let the mixture cool. Transfer the spices to a mortar and pestle or a spice grinder (you can also use a coffee grinder) to grind the spices into a powder.

2. Soak the dried chilis, if using, in water until they become soft. In the meantime, roast the fresh chilis on a baking tray in the oven until they begin to blacken. Remove the chilis from the oven and let them cool.

3. Peel the garlic cloves and place them in a food processor. Add all the other ingredients and process until the mixture is creamy. If the mixture is too thick for your taste, add a little water (½ cup / 1 dl at most) to thin it out.

Turkish Salad,
see recipe on page 59

Taratour (Tahini Sauce with Parsley),
see recipe on page 48

Amba (Pickled Mango),
see recipe on page 55

Tahini Sauce,
see recipe on page 48

Skhug (Yemeni Chili Sauce),
see recipe on page 53

Baba Ganouj,
see recipe on page 56

Eggplant Salad,
see recipe on page 52

EGGPLANT SALAD

Eggplant is such a versatile ingredient. Here it is used in a salad that can be enjoyed both hot and cold.

» **Makes 4 servings**

2 eggplants

salt

neutral oil, such as
    sunflower oil or peanut
    oil, for frying

1 garlic clove

1 bunch parsley

juice from ½ lemon

1. Slice the eggplants into ⅓-inch-thick (1-cm) slices. Place the slices in a colander over a bowl. Salt the slices and let them sit in the colander for about 30 minutes until they begin to sweat. Dab the slices with paper towels to remove any excess moisture.

2. Add oil to a saucepan and place it on the stove over medium-high heat. Once the oil is hot, add the eggplant slices and cook them on both sides until they're completely soft. Remove the eggplant from the pan and drain the excess oil on a plate lined with paper towels.

3. Peel the garlic and chop it roughly with the parsley. To make the dressing, mix the garlic and parsley with the lemon juice in a large bowl. Fold the eggplant into the dressing. Season it with salt to taste and serve.

SKHUG

Skhug (pronounced *suhook*) is an incredibly tasty chili sauce that originated in Yemen. It is very popular in Israel. The flavor varies, depending on the type of chili pepper used. I usually choose a green chili pepper because it adds such a vibrant color.

» Makes about 2 cups (5 dl)

8–10 fresh green chili peppers (3½ ounces / 100 g)

½ cup (1 dl) olive oil

½ cup (1 dl) freshly squeezed lemon juice

3 garlic cloves, peeled

3 teaspoons ground cumin

1 teaspoon ground cardamom

1 teaspoon salt

1 teaspoon ground black pepper

1 bunch cilantro

1. In a bowl, mix the chili peppers, olive oil, and lemon juice. Grate the garlic and add it to the bowl.

2. Add the remaining spices, the salt and pepper, and the cilantro. Using an immersion blender, blend all the ingredients together and serve.

Amba, a pickled mango sauce, is originally from India, but it is also very popular in Iraq. When Iraqi Jews came to Israel, they brought their favorite sauce with them. Amba comes from the word *amra*, which means mango in Sanskrit. To make amba, the mangoes do not have to be ripe. That said, the riper they are, the sweeter the sauce.

AMBA (Pickled Mango)

Amba is a great sauce for grilled dishes and falafel. It can be stored in a clean glass jar in the refrigerator for several weeks. I prefer to puree the sauce until it is smooth before serving it.

» **Makes about 1¼ cups [3 dl]**

4 fresh mangos or
    1½ pounds (675 g)
    frozen diced mango

1 tablespoon salt

1 red or green chili pepper

½ cup (1 dl) neutral oil,
    such as sunflower oil or
    peanut oil

2 tablespoons ground
    fenugreek

1 teaspoon ground
    turmeric

1 teaspoon ground mustard
    seeds

½ cup (1 dl) distilled
    vinegar

1. If you are using fresh mango, peel and cut the fruit and place it in a bowl. If you are using frozen mango, place the cubes in a bowl. Salt the fruit and let it sit for about 1 hour.

2. After 1 hour, chop the chili pepper. Heat the oil in a saucepan. When the oil is hot, add the chili pepper, fenugreek, turmeric, and mustard seeds. Stir constantly over medium heat until the mixture is fragrant.

3. Add the mango to the saucepan and stir until the sauce starts to simmer.

4. Pour the vinegar into the pan. Stir to combine and let the mixture simmer. Remove the pan from the heat. Let the sauce cool before serving.

BABA GANOUJ

This is the king of all eggplant dips. When I was young, my dad used to make baba ganouj with mayonnaise, but, to be authentic, it really should be made with tahini. The dip should also be garlicky, with the fresh taste of lemon.

» **Makes 4 servings**

2 eggplants

3 garlic cloves, peeled

2 tablespoons freshly squeezed lemon juice

1 tablespoon tahini

1 teaspoon salt

olive oil

optional: pomegranate seeds for garnish

1. Preheat the oven to 400°F (200°C). Wrap each of the eggplants in aluminum foil to keep the skin from burning. Roast the eggplants in the oven for about 1 hour.

2. Remove the eggplants from the oven and let them cool. Remove the aluminum foil. The eggplants should be wrinkled and soft.

3. Gently remove the skin from the eggplants and spoon the meat into a large bowl. Add the garlic and lemon juice and mix in the tahini and salt. Using an immersion blender, blend the eggplant mixture until it is smooth.

4. To serve, drizzle the baba ganouj with olive oil, and sprinkle some pomegranate seeds over the top, if desired.

Tip!

You can also garnish this dish with fresh herbs like parsley, cilantro, or mint.

EGGPLANT WITH BELL PEPPER SAUCE

This recipe originated in Falafelbaren, my restaurant in Stockholm. We use bell pepper paste instead of tomato paste in the sauce because some of our guests are allergic to tomatoes. Both vegetables work equally well in this recipe, so choose whichever one you like!

» **Makes 4 servings**

2 eggplants

salt

olive oil

2 garlic cloves

1 large yellow onion

3 tablespoons bell pepper or tomato paste

3 tablespoons water

a splash of freshly squeezed lemon juice

2 teaspoons ground cumin

1 teaspoon ground coriander

1 teaspoon ground black pepper

1. Preheat the oven to 425°F (220°C).

2. Slice the two eggplants in half and then split them again to make 8 pieces. Salt the eggplant, place it on an oiled baking tray, and drizzle it with olive oil.

3. Bake the eggplant in the oven for 40 minutes until it is completely soft.

4. While the eggplant is in the oven, peel and roughly chop the garlic and onion. Add oil to a frying pan over low heat. Once the oil is hot, sauté the garlic and onion until they are soft and golden brown, about 20 minutes. Be careful not to burn them.

5. After 20 minutes, mix the bell pepper paste or tomato paste, water, lemon juice, and spices into the garlic and onion mixture in the pan. Add a little salt to the mixture, if you like, but be aware that bell pepper paste is usually salty, so you may want to taste the mixture before adding more. Stir to combine.

6. After 40 minutes, remove the eggplant from the oven and place it in a large dish. Pour the sauce over the eggplant and gently fold it into the sauce, being careful not to break the eggplant pieces. Once the eggplant is completely covered with the sauce, serve it and enjoy.

SALATA TURKI

Palestine was part of the Ottoman Empire from the sixteenth century until World War I. Among other places, the Ottomans rebuilt Akko, the city where my father's family came from and one of the world's oldest cities, giving it a new wall and new marketplaces. Akko became an important trading place after lying dormant for a few hundred years after the Crusaders lost the city for the last time in 1187. In addition to giving the region better walls and aqueducts, the Ottomans also brought *esmesallad*, which was renamed Salata Turki (Turkish Salad).

» **Makes 4 servings**

1 yellow onion, peeled and finely chopped

2 garlic cloves, peeled and finely chopped

4 tomatoes, finely chopped

2 fresh red or green chili peppers (whatever kind you like!), finely chopped

1 bunch parsley, finely chopped

1 tablespoon freshly squeezed lemon juice

2 teaspoons pomegranate syrup

2 teaspoons bell pepper paste

1 tablespoon olive oil

1 teaspoon ground sumac

a pinch of salt

2 teaspoons chopped fresh mint

1. Combine the onion, garlic, tomatoes, chili peppers, and parsley in a bowl.

2. Add the lemon juice, pomegranate syrup, bell pepper paste, and olive oil to bowl. Stir together the ingredients until they are well combined. Season the salad with the ground sumac, salt, and mint.

MUHAMMARA

Muhammara is a spicy, creamy, and delicious dip that pairs nicely with many different dishes. If you do not have an immersion blender, you can simply mince the ingredients and then stir them all together into a smooth mixture that still has a little texture.

» **Makes 4 servings**

6 red bell peppers

about 2 tablespoons neutral oil, such as sunflower oil or peanut oil

½ cup (1 dl) walnuts

1 teaspoon chili powder

2 teaspoons paprika

2 garlic cloves, peeled

1 tablespoon freshly squeezed lemon juice

1 tablespoon pomegranate syrup

salt to taste

optional: pomegranate seeds for garnish

1. Preheat the oven to 400°F (200°C).

2. Place the bell peppers on a baking tray, drizzle them with the oil, and bake in the oven for about 30 minutes. After 30 minutes, remove the peppers from the oven and let them cool.

3. While the peppers are cooling, toast the walnuts in a dry frying pan. Once the nuts are golden brown, set them aside to cool and then coarsely chop them.

4. When the peppers are cool, remove the cores. Using an immersion blender, blend the peppers with the rest of the ingredients, including the chopped walnuts, until the mixture is smooth but still has some texture.

5. To serve, spoon the dip into a bowl and top with fresh pomegranate seeds, if you like.

Muhammara comes from the Arabic word for the color red.

VEGETARIAN DISHES

Falafel

FALAFEL

The Middle East is the epicenter of the debate over falafel: who makes the best falafel and who owns it. It's likely that falafel originated in Egypt, but since then it has spread—and been enjoyed by many—throughout the Middle East and around the world. Falafel can be made with either chickpeas or fava beans or a mixture of the two.

When you order falafel from a restaurant, it should be fried-to-order and served with tahini sauce or taratour (see recipes on page 48). Falafel can vary in flavor, depending on the spices used; for example, if fresh herbs are used, the falafel will look dark after frying. Dried herbs will result in a golden-brown color. In the Middle East falafel is served in a pita with sliced tomatoes, pickles, some fresh mint leaf, and tahini sauce.

The most important step while preparing falafel is to soak dried chickpeas rather than use canned chickpeas, which have been pre-boiled. If possible, use a mill for grinding the chickpeas, as it provides the best results. The grinder plate should have a hole size of $\frac{3}{16}$ inch (4.5 mm). The finer the holes, the smoother the falafel mixture, but it will also be less crispy. If you use $\frac{3}{16}$ inches (4.5 mm), make sure to grind the mixture twice for the correct consistency. You can also use a food processor—just be careful not to make the batter completely smooth.

There are different techniques to make falafel balls. The easiest way is to simply use your hands or a small ice cream scoop.

» **Makes 6 servings**

18 ounces (500 g) dried
   chickpeas

2 small yellow onions or
   1 big yellow onion,
   about 3½ ounces (100 g)

2 garlic cloves

1 bunch cilantro

1 bunch parsley

1 scallion

2 fresh chili peppers

Tip!

If you have leftover falafel batter, you can keep it in the refrigerator for a few days. You can also freeze it and use it later.

1. Soak the chickpeas in water for 9–12 hours or overnight. Keep in mind that they will swell to almost three times their original size, so use a lot of water to soak them. After the chickpeas have been thoroughly soaked, drain them in a colander or strainer.

2. Peel and roughly chop the onion and garlic.

2 tablespoons ground
  cumin

½ tablespoon ground
  coriander

1 tablespoon salt

½ cup (1 dl) water

1 teaspoon baking soda

½ gallon (2 l) oil, such as
  sunflower oil or peanut
  oil, for frying

— *YOU NEED*

1 grinding mill or food
  processor

1 deep saucepan for frying
  or a deep fryer

perforated ladle or strainer
  with handle

— *FOR SERVING*

pita bread, see recipe
  on page 33

Jerusalem salad, see
  recipe on page 103

skhug, see recipe on
  page 53

fried potatoes, see
  recipe on page 110

pickles

tahini sauce, see recipe
  on page 48

3. To make the batter, combine the chickpeas, onions, garlic, cilantro, parsley, scallion, and chili peppers. Put the mixture through a grinding mill on the finest setting, or use a food processor. Process the mixture in batches, pulsing each for about 35 seconds or until the ingredients are finely chopped but hold together. Mix in the dry spices, salt, water, and baking soda.

4. In a deep saucepan, heat the oil to 365°F (185°C).

5. *To make the falafel balls:* Use a large spoon or a small ice cream scoop to form about 1 tablespoon of the batter into a small ball. Gently place the falafel balls in the hot oil, being careful not to crowd the pan. Wait a few seconds before moving the falafel around in the pan so that the edges do not break off. After 3 or 4 minutes, when the falafel is golden brown on all sides and cooked through, use a perforated ladle or strainer to remove it from the oil. Set the falafel on a large plate or platter covered with paper towels to absorb excess oil. Serve immediately with pita bread, Jerusalem salad, skhug, fried potatoes, pickles, and tahini sauce.

Choose the right oil!

A neutral oil like sunflower oil, peanut oil, or rapeseed oil, does not add flavor to fried food. Many people in the Mediterranean, however, use olive oil—a choice that is much debated. Those who argue against olive oil point out that it has a relatively low smoke point, but you rarely need a higher temperature (or an oil with a higher smoke point) to fry most food. When I fry potatoes, for example, I like to use a mix of olive oil and rapeseed oil, which gives the potatoes a lovely flavor!

Before you fry anything, examine the oil. Different oils can handle a range of temperatures and it is important that the oil never smokes during frying. If the oil smells rancid or starts to foam upon heating, discard it. To discard used oil properly, do not pour it down the sink. Instead, wait until the oil has cooled, then put it in a nonbreakable container with a lid, recycle it, or throw it in the garbage.

SWEDISH FALAFEL

I was in Paris when I made falafel for the first time, after having discovered the aroma of freshly baked falafel at a shop on the Rue des Rosiers. When I got home to the small apartment where I was staying, I looked around for the equipment I needed to make falafel. The only thing I could find that was similar to a mill was a garlic press. I pushed chickpeas through the press, a few at a time, followed by the garlic and onion. Finally, I chopped the coriander and parsley and mixed everything together into a batter. I don't remember if the falafel was good. The only thing I remember was pushing 2¼ pounds (1 kg) of chickpeas through a single garlic press.

The second time I made falafel was at the Peace & Love festival in Borlänge. At that time, it was Sweden's largest festival, and a good friend and I planned to sell five thousand servings of various dishes. My friend, my brother, and I misled our little brothers into doing a lot more work than they anticipated. Plus we overestimated how much falafel we'd sell, so the whole enterprise was a bit of an economic disaster. This recipe for falafel uses yellow peas instead of chickpeas and wild garlic instead of coriander. The result is a different—and delicious—take on the original recipe!

» **Makes 6 servings**

18 ounces (500 g) yellow
    split peas soaked for
    at least 4 hours

2 yellow onions

1 bunch dill

1 bunch parsley

1 scallion

3½ ounces (100 g) wild
    garlic

1 tablespoon salt

½ cup (1 dl) water

1 teaspoon baking soda

oil for frying

• To make this falafel, follow the instructions for basic falafel on page 65.

Souq al rous is a Russian flea market in the old part of Akko, in northern Israel, created by Soviet immigrants in the 1980s. Here, they sold goods that they had brought with them from their homeland. Today the market continues, but the nesting dolls (matryoshki) and fabrics have been replaced by vegetables, meat, and everything in between.

MOROCCAN CARROT SALAD

There are many variations of this salad. For example, you can boil the carrots instead of roasting them in the oven, but I prefer to roast the carrots on high heat so that they caramelize a bit. A simple trick for ensuring the carrots don't lose their firmness is to cool them down in cold water or an ice bath immediately after roasting them in the oven. This will prevent them from cooking any further.

» **Makes 4 servings**

2¼ **pounds (1 kg) carrots**

3 **garlic cloves, peeled and chopped**

1 **bunch cilantro, chopped**

1 **tablespoon freshly squeezed lemon juice**

2 **teaspoons ground cumin**

1 **teaspoon salt**

1 **tablespoon harissa**

2 **tablespoons olive oil**

1. Preheat the oven to 425°F (220°C).

2. Wash the carrots.

3. Place the garlic and cilantro in a bowl. Add the lemon juice, cumin, salt, and harissa and mix to combine. Add a little more harissa if you prefer more heat.

4. Place the uncooked carrots on a baking sheet, drizzle with oil, and roast in the oven for about 15 minutes. The carrots will take on a darker color as they caramelize. Remove the carrots from the oven and let them cool.

5. Cut the carrots into rounds and place them in the bowl with the spices. Mix together all the ingredients, using your hands, making sure to work the sauce into the carrots.

OKRA WITH VERMICELLI RICE

If you can't find fresh okra, you can buy it frozen in most well-stocked grocery stores. My grand-mother always made this dish for us—and always cooked the garlic separately in a lot of olive oil, which she then poured into the simmering okra. In Arabic, this is called "making a tashi." In Palestine, people prefer to use small baby okra; in other countries, some people prefer to use larger okra pods. For this recipe, you can use whatever kind you can find.

» **Makes 4 servings**

— *FOR THE STEW*

olive oil for frying

1 pound (400 g) fresh or frozen okra

18 ounces (500 g) canned crushed tomatoes

4 tablespoons tomato paste

⅔ cup (2 dl) of water

2 teaspoons baharat, see recipe on page 26

salt

freshly ground black pepper

5 garlic cloves

optional: **cherry tomatoes as garnish**

— *FOR THE VERMICELLI RICE*

½ cup (1 dl) vermicelli

olive oil or butter for frying

1¼ cups (3 dl) basmati rice

1 teaspoon salt

cold water

— *TO MAKE THE STEW*

1. Pour some oil into a frying pan, enough to cover the bottom of the pan, and sear the okra for a few minutes over medium-high heat, until tender and lightly browned.

2. Add the crushed tomatoes, tomato paste, and water to the pan. Mix in the baharat, salt, and pepper, and simmer until the okra is soft, about 30 minutes.

3. Peel and chop the garlic. In a separate frying pan, add enough oil to saturate the garlic and still have enough oil in which to fry it. When the garlic has turned golden brown, add it—and the oil in which it was fried—to the stew.

— *TO MAKE THE VERMICELLI RICE*

1. In a separate pan, cook the vermicelli in a little oil (and butter, if you like). Add the rice to the pan, stirring it constantly so that it doesn't burn.

* *Note:* Vermicelli is a thin, short pasta that is often served, mixed with rice, in Middle Eastern dishes. These days you can find it in most well-stocked grocery stores.

2. Add the salt to the vermicelli-rice mixture and cover it with cold water. Allow the water to come to a boil and then lower the heat. Cover the pan and let the mixture simmer for about 10 minutes.

3. Remove the pan from the heat and let the vermicelli-rice rest in the pan for another 10 minutes. Then fluff the mixture with a fork and serve it with the stew.

FREEKEH WITH MUSHROOMS

Freekeh is made from durum wheat and has been cultivated in the Fertile Crescent (an area extending from Egypt to Iraq) for several thousand years. To make freekeh—a word derived from the Arabic word *farek*, which means "to rub"—first you must harvest the wheat while it is still green and quickly smoke it until it is dry. The wheat casings are then rubbed off. The process results in a slightly smoky-flavored grain. And, as with all ancient grains, freekeh is very nutritious and high in protein.

» **Makes 4 servings**

1 yellow onion

4 garlic cloves

olive oil for frying

8 ounces (250 g) mushrooms

1¾ cups (4 dl) freekeh

1¼ cups (3 dl) light beer

3½ ounces (100 g) grated Parmesan cheese

1 tablespoon za'atar, see recipe on page 29

1 teaspoon salt

freshly ground black pepper

1. Peel and chop the onion and garlic. In a frying pan, place some of the oil over medium-high heat. When the oil is hot, add the onion and garlic and cook them until they're soft. Slice the mushrooms, then add them to the pan and continue to fry the mixture until the mushrooms are tender.

2. Rinse the freekeh and pour it into the pan, stirring to combine it with the grain and vegetables. Add the beer to the pan and simmer until the liquid has almost evaporated.

3. Mix in the Parmesan cheese. Season the freekeh with the za'atar, salt, and pepper to taste before serving.

Tip!

Freekeh can be used in many dishes as an alternative to rice, couscous, or bulgur. It cooks quickly, in about 20 minutes. If you can't find freekeh, you can use barley or wheatberries instead.

HARICOTS VERTS IN TOMATO SAUCE

This recipe for green beans in tomato sauce is a riff on fasolakia, a traditional Greek dish. In Palestine, people often use fresh, tender string beans, such as haricots verts, to make the dish. This recipe doesn't include many ingredients, but it is delicious. In fact, my brother claims that it is his favorite food. He usually enjoys it with glass of white wine, simply because everything is better with wine.

» **Makes 4 servings**

1 yellow onion

olive oil for frying

¼ cup (¼ dl) white wine

6 tomatoes

2 tablespoons tomato paste

½ cup (1 dl) water

handful of bay leaves

3 garlic cloves

18 ounces (500 g) haricots verts

1. Peel and chop the onion. Pour some olive oil into a frying pan and sauté the onion until it becomes transparent.

2. Pour the white wine into the pan. Quickly cut the tomatoes into segments and place them in the pan. Add the tomato paste, water, and bay leaves.

3. Bring the sauce to a boil. Let it continue to boil for 15 minutes.

4. While the sauce cooks, peel and chop the garlic. Add some olive oil to another pan and sauté the garlic until it is lightly golden. Add the garlic—and the oil in which it was cooked—to the pan of hot tomato sauce. Add the haricots verts and cook them in the sauce until they are tender but still retain their texture and bright color. Serve with vermicelli rice (see recipe on page 74).

FATTOUSH

It is said that fattoush, essentially a bread salad, originated in northern Lebanon. You can use stale pita to make the croutons. Ingredients in fattoush vary from place to place. This recipe packs a refreshing lemony punch, along with the bracing flavors of ground sumac and portulaca, a wild herb that grows in the Middle East (and in many other parts of the world). You can use various kinds of cucumbers in fattoush, depending on what is in season or on hand. Pickling cucumbers, like Kirby, are a popular choice in the US.

» **Makes 4 servings**

— *FOR THE CROUTONS*

pita bread, see recipe on page 33

olive oil

za'atar, see recipe on page 29

— *FOR THE SALAD*

1 bunch radishes

1 shallot

1 scallion

4 tomatoes

4–5 small cucumbers, such as Kirby, or 1 plain big cucumber

1 bunch mint

1 bunch parsley

1 bunch purslane, if you can get a hold of it

1 head romaine lettuce

1. Preheat the oven to 350°F (180°C).

2. *To make the croutons:* Cube the pita bread into 1-inch (2–3-cm) pieces and arrange them on a baking tray. Drizzle with olive oil and toss to coat evenly. Toast the bread in the oven until it turns golden brown, about 10 minutes. Remove the tray and season the bread with za'atar. Set it aside.

3. Set out a large bowl for the salad. Julienne the radishes and peel and thinly slice the shallot. Finely chop the scallion. Dice the tomatoes and cucumbers. Finely chop the mint and parsley and slice the romaine into ¼-inch (1-cm) strips. Toss all the ingredients in the bowl.

4. For the dressing, peel and mince the garlic (or put it through a garlic press) and combine it, in a bowl, with the olive oil, lemon juice, ground sumac, and salt. Pour the dressing over the salad and toss to combine.

5. Cut the halloumi into bite-size cubes. Place some olive oil in a heavy skillet over medium heat. When hot, add the halloumi and cook for a few minutes until it has turned a nice golden brown color on all sides.

FOR THE DRESSING

2 garlic cloves

2 tablespoons olive oil

juice of 1 lemon

1 teaspoon ground sumac

a pinch of salt

1 package halloumi,
  about 6 ounces (180 g)

olive oil

pomegranate syrup

6. Top the salad with the fried halloumi and pita croutons. Drizzle some pomegranate syrup over the top and serve.

HUMMUS

Hummus, the Middle East's most famous dish, is eaten throughout the Levant (Syria, Lebanon, Palestine, Israel, Jordan, and others) and has spread across much of the world.

In Arabic, *hummus* means "chickpeas," but it's also the name of a dish made of cooked chickpeas and tahini. There are two prerequisites for making great hummus. First, the chickpeas should be cooked until they are soft—just on the verge of breaking—but not broken, and you must use really good tahini.

A simple rule to follow when shopping for tahini is to buy the most expensive tahini you can find that has Arabic text on the label. The color should be light and the consistency smooth. Some products on the market are labeled "tahini," but they're actually made from crushed sesame seeds. If you use this type of tahini, your hummus will not be smooth and creamy, the way it should be.

Adding baking soda to the water, when cooking chickpeas, will both save time and help the chickpeas soften. If you don't use baking soda, add at least one more hour of cooking time. Cooking time may also vary, depending on the variety of chickpea. Organic varieties, for example, have a thinner skin (and a sweeter taste) than other types of chickpeas and will cook a little faster.

Hummus is eaten both as a side dish and a main dish, for example, with fried meatballs, shawarma (see recipe on page 120), or mushrooms.

HUMMUS

7 ounces (200 g) dried
   chickpeas

water

1 teaspoon baking soda

½ cup (1 dl) boiled
   chickpea water

2–3 garlic cloves

½ cup (1 dl) tahini

juice of 1 lemon

salt

— *FOR SERVING*

½ cup (1 dl) canola or
   olive oil, for serving

tomatoes

onions

pita bread, see recipe
   on page 33

optional: mint tea, see
   recipe on page 168

1. Soak the chickpeas for at least 8 hours or overnight.

2. After soaking the chickpeas, drain them in a colander and transfer them to a large pot. Fill the pot with a generous amount of water, add the baking soda, and bring the water to a boil. When it boils, reduce the heat to a simmer. Cook the chickpeas for 1–1½ hours or until they are soft and have the consistency of boiled potatoes.

3. While the chickpeas are cooking, white foam or scum will form on the surface of the water and the skin on the chickpeas may loosen. Use a spoon to skim the scum off the top. Use a slotted spoon or a small handheld strainer to remove skins that float to the surface.

4. When the chickpeas have finished cooking and are soft, drain them in a colander. Pour most of the water out of the pot, but save a few cups for blending the chickpeas. Save ½ cup (1 dl) of whole chickpeas for garnishing the hummus, if you like.

5. Add the chickpeas to a food processor and pulse for a few minutes. Add about ½ cup (1 dl) of the reserved cooking water. The advantage of mixing chickpeas while they're hot is that it's easier to get a smooth purée. Allow the mixture to cool.

6. Peel the garlic cloves. Add them to the chickpea mixture and run the food processor for a few more minutes to make it completely smooth. Pour in the tahini and mix. Add the lemon juice and process for a while longer. This will make the hummus fluffy. Season with salt to taste.

7. To serve, scoop the hummus onto the middle of a plate and give it a swirl. Drizzle plenty of olive oil over the top along with a few of the reserved whole chickpeas and a squeeze of lemon juice, if you like. Enjoy the hummus with slices of tomato and raw onion, pita bread, and a hot cup of mint tea.

MSABAHA

Msabaha is a lot like hummus, but it is still very much its own dish. To make msabaha, the chickpeas aren't blended to produce a smooth consistency like hummus. Instead, they are mixed together with the other ingredients by hand, which gives the dish its unique texture. If you use canned chickpeas, be sure to boil them for about 20 minutes so that they soften up.

» **Makes 4 servings**

2 cups (5 dl) cooked
   (or canned) chickpeas

1 bunch parsley, for
   garnish

1 bunch mint, for garnish

½ cup (1 dl) tahini

½ cup (1 dl) freshly
   squeezed lemon juice

½ cup (1 dl) cold water

2 garlic cloves, peeled

1 teaspoon salt

olive oil for serving

pita bread, see recipe
   on page 33

olives

1. Cook the chickpeas according to the recipe for hummus on page 84. After draining the cooked chickpeas, set them aside (do not blend them in a mixer).

2. While the chickpeas are cooking, finely chop the parsley and mint. Set aside.

3. In a bowl, stir together the tahini, lemon juice, and cold water. Press the garlic through a garlic press and add it to the tahini mixture. Add the salt and stir.

4. Add the chickpeas and mix thoroughly, leaving some of the chickpeas whole, which will give the dish a chunkier consistency than hummus.

5. Garnish the msabaha with the parsley and mint, and serve it with a generous drizzle of good olive oil. Warm pita bread and olives make great accompaniments to this dish.

Beans and pulses are staples in the Middle East—cultivated for thousands of years, they are cheap and packed with nutrition.

FOUL

Foul (or ful, as it is also known) has been overshadowed by hummus in some places, but in the Middle East people actually eat more foul than hummus. In fact, some workplaces prohibit their employees from eating foul for lunch because it is common to go into a foul coma if you eat too much of it.

Like chickpeas, foul (fava beans) are a staple in Middle Eastern kitchens. They are eaten in different ways—sometimes mashed, like hummus, mixed with chickpeas, or prepared in a soup. No matter what, foul always includes raw onion, lemon juice, and olive oil; fancier preparations might also include fresh mint, cilantro, tahini sauce, or yogurt.

The kind of foul we make at Falafelbaren, my restaurant in Stockholm, is inspired by Syria, where you often eat it as a soup. In the world of foul, there are endless possibilities for developing wonderful broths. For example, why not use the cooking water from chickpeas to enrich your Foul?

» **Makes 4 servings**

— *FOR THE FOUL*

1 yellow onion

olive oil for frying

about 2½ cups (6 dl) water

1 teaspoon salt

1 teaspoon ground cumin

1 teaspoon ground
  coriander

2 cups cooked or
  canned fava beans,
  about 16 ounces
  (400 g)

1. Peel and slice the onion.

2. Place the oil in a saucepan and sauté half of the onion. Pour in the water, add the salt, and bring to a boil. Add the cumin and ground coriander to the mixture.

3. Rinse the fava beans and pour them into the saucepan. Simmer for 10 minutes over low heat. Remove the parsley leaves from the stems. Discard the stems and coarsely chop the leaves.

4. Assemble the pickled turnips and tahini sauce for accompaniments.

— FOR SERVING

1 bunch parsley

pickled turnips, see recipe
   on page 111

tahini sauce, see recipe on
   page 48

4 hard-boiled eggs

olive oil

lemon slices

pita bread, see recipe on
   page 33

5. Place the foul in a deep bowl. Top it with the parsley, the other half of the raw onion, boiled eggs, and turnips. Drizzle the dish with tahini sauce, olive oil, and a generous squeeze of juice from the lemon slices. Serve the foul with pita bread.

TABBOULI

It was not until my friend Jann made tabbouli for me that I understood just how much a person can truly love one dish. Jann eats tabbouli just about every day. In his hunt for fresh parsley, he goes to several stores. When he gets home, he rinses the parsley, removes any imperfections, and makes small bouquets. He then places the bouquets in small plastic bags that look like balloons. The air in the bags helps keep the parsley fresh. The uncooked bulgur in this recipe soaks up all the juices from the vegetables, keeping the tabbouli fresh longer as well as adding a nice texture.

10½ ounces (300 g / about
    2 bunches) flat-leaf
    parsley, stems removed,
    washed, dried well, and
    finely chopped

2 ounces (50 g / about
    two bunches) mint,
    stems removed,
    washed, dried well,
    and finely chopped

4–5 Roma tomatoes

1 large cucumber or
    similar amount of
    mini (or pickling)
    cucumbers

1 small yellow onion or
    2 shallots, peeled and
    chopped

1 scallion, chopped

1 fresh green chili pepper,
    chopped

½ cup (1 dl) bulgur wheat

zest + juice from 1 lemon

salt

olive oil

romaine lettuce, for serving

1. Put the prepared parsley and mint in a bowl and set it aside.

2. Finely dice the tomatoes into small cubes. The simplest way is to cut the tomatoes into ¼-inch-thick (½-cm) slices and then dice them. Do the same with the cucumber.

3. Add the prepared onion or shallots, scallion, chili pepper, and uncooked bulgur to a large bowl.

4. Thoroughly combine all the ingredients. Add the lemon zest and juice and salt to taste. Drizzle olive oil over the top. Spoon the tabbouli into the romaine lettuce leaves and eat them like tacos, if you like.

LENTILS WITH YOGURT SAUCE

To make this dish, you'll need to prepare all the components separately. I suggest starting with the yogurt sauce. Don't be intimidated by all the onions in this recipe! They will be sautéed until they're heavenly sweet, and you'll wish you'd made even more. A big frying pan makes it easier to sauté the onions.

» **Makes 4 servings**

— *FOR THE YOGURT SAUCE*

1¾ cups (4 dl) plain yogurt

1 cucumber, sliced

1 garlic clove, pressed in a
 garlic press or minced

salt

— *FOR THE LENTILS*

⅔ cup (2 dl) green lentils
 or black "beluga" lentils

1 bay leaf

a pinch of baharat, see
 recipe on page 26

4 yellow onions

oil for frying

⅔ cup (2 dl) black rice

4 cardamom pods

salt

freshly ground black
 pepper

1. Pour the yogurt into a coffee filter and drain in the fridge over a bowl for at least two hours.

2. Drain the sliced cucumber in a colander for about 20 minutes. Mix the cucumber with the drained yogurt and garlic in a bowl. Season the mixture with salt to taste.

3. Fill a saucepan with salted water. Add the lentils, bay leaf, and baharat and bring the water to a boil. Cook the lentils until they are soft (cooking times may vary, depending on the lentils you choose). Drain the lentils and set them aside.

4. While the lentils are cooking, peel and slice two of the onions. Add oil to a frying pan. When the oil is hot, sauté the onions over medium to low heat until they are soft and the onions start to slowly caramelize. Add the rice to the pan with as much water as the package indicates. Add the cardamom pods and boil the rice until it has absorbed all the water.

5. Peel and slice the remaining two onions. Heat some oil in a frying pan and sauté the onions over medium heat until they are caramelized. Remove the onions from the pan and drain them on paper towels.

6. In a large frying pan, heat more oil. Fry the rice, add the lentils, and stir. Top the mixture with the caramelized onions, season with salt and pepper, and serve with the cool yogurt sauce.

SHAKSHUKA

Originally from North Africa, shakshuka is an amazing dish in which eggs are poached in a delicious, spicy stew of tomatoes, onion, and chili peppers. It is perfect for a leisurely weekend brunch, served with hot pita bread and hummus. When I make shakshuka, I always begin by cooking the onion over low heat for a really long time. The caramelized onions bring out the sweetness of the tomatoes. For best results, use a frying pan or saucepan with a lid.

» Makes 4 servings

1 yellow onion

olive oil for frying

3 garlic cloves

5 tomatoes

2 small, fresh, hot chili peppers (such as jalapeño, serrano, or Fresno), stems, seeds, and ribs removed

1 tablespoon ground cumin

1 teaspoon ground coriander

1 teaspoon ground black pepper

1 teaspoon salt

1 tablespoon harissa (or more, if you like the heat), tomato paste, or bell pepper paste

½ cup (1 dl) light beer or water

1 bunch cilantro

4 fresh eggs

1. Peel and dice the onion. Heat olive oil in a large skillet or saucepan over high heat until the oil starts to shimmer. Add the onion to the pan and fry it for 15 minutes, preferably covered, stirring occasionally.

2. Peel and grate or chop the garlic and add it to the saucepan. Cook the mixture for 5 minutes.

3. Coarsely chop the tomatoes and thinly slice the peppers. Add the tomatoes and peppers to the onion mixture. Stir to combine. Add the spices, salt, pepper, and harissa or tomato paste. Pour in the beer (it's okay to use water, but beer is more fun). Bring the sauce to a boil and then reduce the heat to low. Let the sauce simmer for about 15 minutes. Season with salt and pepper to taste.

4. Chop the cilantro. Reserve some for garnish, if you like, and mix the rest into the sauce.

5. When the stew is ready, the shakshuka should be thick enough to make four shallow wells with the back of a large spoon. Break an egg into each of the wells, being careful not to break the egg yolks. Spoon a little of the sauce over the egg whites, leaving the yolks exposed. Put the lid on the pan and cook the

— *FOR SERVING*

**pita bread, see recipe on
page 33**

**hummus, see recipe on
page 84**

sauce over very low heat for 5–8 minutes, until the eggs are cooked. Remove the pan from the heat and sprinkle the reserved cilantro over the top, if using.

6. Serve the shakshuka with warm pita bread and hummus.

SABICH

This dish, a favorite of Iraqi Jews, is the perfect egg sandwich. Traditionally, it is prepared before the Sabbath, and thus, when served, the ingredients are cold and the eggs are hard-boiled. You can also fry the eggs if you like, but then you'd be breaking with tradition.

» Makes 4 servings

4 eggs

1 eggplant

salt

1 cauliflower head

olive oil for frying

— FOR SERVING

pita bread, see recipe on
    page 33, or flat bread

hummus, see recipe on
    page 84

tahini sauce, see recipe
    on page 48

amba, see recipe on
    page 55

optional: skhug, see recipe
    on page 53

Jerusalem salad, see recipe
    on page 103

1. Boil the eggs.

2. Slice the eggplant into ¼-inch (½-cm) rounds and salt them generously. Let the eggplant drain in a colander over a bowl for 10–15 minutes until they begin to release their liquid.

3. In the meantime, break the cauliflower into small florets.

4. After the eggplant has drained, pat it dry with paper towels to absorb any excess liquid.

5. Prepare a frying pan with a decent amount of oil. Fry the eggplant slices on each side until they turn golden brown. Set them aside. Do the same with the cauliflower. Set it aside.

6. To assemble the sandwich, fill a pita or flat bread with the eggplant, cauliflower, boiled egg, hummus, tahini, and amba. Top with a little skhug if you like it hot. Serve with Jerusalem salad.

IL HARA OSBAU
—(The One that Burns the Finger)

Unfortunately, this dish will not become an international hit because of its name—*Il hara osbau*, or "the one that burns the finger." The dish received this colorful name because it is so delicious that it's impossible not to eat it, even when it is so hot that it burns your fingers. The dish comes from Syria and should you be invited by a Syrian family to join them for a dinner of "the one that burns the finger," you'll know just how popular a guest you are. Traditionally, the dish is made with fresh egg pasta, but here I've replaced it with potato gnocchi. You can also eat this dish cold . . . if you don't want to burn your fingers!

» **Makes 4 servings**

pita bread, see recipe on
    page 33

olive oil

salt

2 big yellow onions

1¼ cups (3 dl) black or
    "beluga" lentils or
    something similar

water

2 teaspoons ground cumin

¼ cup (½ dl) pomegranate
    syrup

5 ounces (150 g) fresh
    spinach

5 garlic cloves

1 bunch cilantro

4 portions potato gnocchi
    (or any short pasta)

1. Preheat the oven to 350°F (180°C). Cut the pita bread into about ¾-inch (2-cm) pieces. Drizzle the pieces of bread with oil, sprinkle them with salt, arrange them on a baking tray, and toast them in the oven until they are crisp.

2. Peel and slice the onions. Pour a little olive oil into a saucepan and sauté the onions for at least 10–15 minutes, until they have caramelized. Set the onions aside.

3. Rinse the lentils and put them in a large pot. Add enough water to cover the lentils by about ¾ inch (2 cm). Bring the water to a boil. Remove any foam or scum that forms on the surface. Lower the heat and let the lentils simmer for about 10 minutes.

4. After 10 minutes, add the cumin, salt to taste, and half of the caramelized onions. Add the pomegranate syrup. Stir to combine and continue to simmer. Taste the lentils and add more salt or cumin if needed. Rinse the spinach and set it aside.

5. Peel and finely chop the garlic. Finely chop the cilantro and set it aside. Heat enough oil for frying in a small frying pan. When the oil is hot, sauté the garlic and cilantro over high heat. When the garlic is golden, pour half of it into the lentil stew. Set aside the rest. Add the gnocchi and about half of the spinach to the stew and gently stir it in. When the gnocchi is cooked, the dish is ready.

6. To serve, top the dish with the remaining caramelized onion, garlic, spinach, and the toasted pita.

JERUSALEM SALAD

This salad is available in various forms all over the Mediterranean and has a number of different names: the Turks call it *Salata Çoban* (shepherd's salad, a classic in Turkey); the Arabs call it Arabian salad; and the Israelis call it Israeli salad. No matter what you call it, the dish basically consists of tomatoes, cucumber, onion, some garlic, lemon juice, and fresh herbs. In the interest of Middle Eastern peace, we call it Jerusalem salad. Eat it with everything.

» **Makes 4 servings**

4 tomatoes

1 cucumber

1 yellow onion

1 bunch parsley

1 bunch mint

1 garlic clove

2 tablespoons freshly
   squeezed lemon juice

1 tablespoon olive oil

salt

freshly ground black
   pepper

1. Dice the tomatoes and cucumber. Peel and chop the onion and chop the parsley and mint. Mix all the ingredients in a bowl.

2. Peel the garlic and mince it. In a small bowl, whisk together the lemon juice, oil, and garlic to make the dressing. Pour the dressing over the salad ingredients and toss to combine. Add salt and pepper to taste and serve.

BULGUR AND TOMATOES
(*Smeedeh wa Bandora*)

In many ways, this dish epitomizes the simple life. When my dad was a kid, his family ate bulgur and tomatoes several times a week. Bulgur, or *burghul*, as it is called in Arabic, is wheat that has been parboiled, dried, and cracked, making it quick to cook. It has been eaten in the Middle East for several thousand years and is valued to this day for its long shelf life and versatility.

» **Makes 4 servings**

18 ounces (500 g) coarse (not fine) bulgur

1 medium yellow onion

olive oil for frying

6 whole tomatoes

1 tablespoon tomato paste

1 teaspoon baharat, see recipe on page 26

1 bottle (11 ounces / 33 cl) light beer

salt

freshly ground black pepper

parsley, chopped for garnish

1. Thoroughly rinse the bulgur and set it aside. Peel and finely chop the onion. Heat the oil in a large skillet. Add the onion and sauté until it becomes soft.

2. Dice the tomatoes and add them to the frying pan with the onion. Cover and simmer until the tomatoes become soft. Add the tomato paste and baharat to the pan and stir to combine.

3. Add the bulgur and beer to the pan and stir. Let the tomato sauce cook with the bulgur for about 10 minutes. Add water if necessary. Season with salt and pepper to taste. Garnish with parsley and serve.

ROASTED EGGPLANT WITH TOMATO AND CILANTRO SALAD

The idea for this dish came to me one day when I was feeling sorry for my colleagues, who had been eating falafel for lunch every day for several years. If you want to make this dish a bit more filling, add some crumbled feta cheese.

» **Makes 4 servings as an appetizer or side dish**

2 large eggplants, halved lengthwise

salt

neutral oil, such as canola

½ yellow onion

4 Roma tomatoes

1 fresh chili pepper (such as jalapeño, serrano, or Fresno), stems, seeds, and ribs removed

1 bunch cilantro

2 garlic cloves

1 tablespoon freshly squeezed lemon juice

freshly ground black pepper

1. Deeply score the cut sides of the eggplants and salt them generously. Let the eggplant sit in a colander and drain for about 30 minutes.

2. Preheat the oven to 425°F (220°C).

3. Place the eggplant on an oiled baking tray. Drizzle the eggplant with oil and bake it in the oven for 20–30 minutes.

4. When the eggplant is done, remove the tray from the oven. Carefully transfer the eggplant to a serving dish or plate so that it doesn't fall apart. Set it aside to cool.

5. *To make the salad:* Peel and dice the onion; coarsely chop the tomatoes and chili pepper, and chop the cilantro. Combine in a bowl. Peel and mince the garlic or squeeze it through a press and add it to the salad ingredients. Pour the lemon juice over the salad and stir to combine. Season with salt and pepper to taste.

6. To serve, spoon some of the salad over each of the eggplant halves.

SWEET POTATO FRIES

I prefer my fried sweet potatoes without the skin, so I peel them. The potato flour will help the sweet potatoes become crispy and also protect them from burning in the hot oil. They don't stay crispy for long, though, so eat them quickly!

» Makes 4 servings

10½ ounces (300 g / about 2 medium) sweet potatoes

cold water

¼ cup (½ dl) potato flour

neutral oil, such as canola

a pinch of salt

a pinch of ground cumin

1. Peel and cut the sweet potatoes in half lengthwise. Lay the potato halves cut side down and slice them lengthwise into ½-inch-thick (1.25-cm) slices. Stack the slices evenly and then cut them lengthwise again into ¼-inch-thick (1-cm) strips. Place the sweet potatoes in a large bowl of cold water for about 1 hour.

2. After 1 hour, remove the potatoes from the water and dry the strips with a towel. Place the potatoes in a large bowl and mix in the potato flour.

3. Fill a large saucepan with 2 inches (5 cm) of oil and place it on the stove over high heat. When the oil is hot, about 350°F (180°C), add the potato strips to the pan, a few at a time (you may have to fry them in batches). Fry the sweet potatoes, stirring occasionally, until they brown, about 5 minutes. Transfer the sweet potato fries to a baking sheet lined with paper towels, sprinkle them with the salt and cumin, and serve them while they're hot and crispy.

FRIED POTATOES

Batatama'liye, fried potatoes, are popular in many countries, not least in the Middle East. These delicious potatoes won't be as crispy as french fries, but their softness makes them ideal to serve with saucy dishes.

» **Makes 4 servings**

10½ ounces (300 g / about 2 medium) baking potatoes (Russets are a good choice)

cold water

neutral oil, such as canola

salt

1. Slice the potatoes in half lengthwise. Lay the potato halves cut side down and slice them lengthwise into ½-inch-thick (1.25-cm) slices. Stack the slices evenly and then cut them lengthwise again, into ¼-inch-thick (1-cm) strips. Place the potatoes in a large bowl of cold water for about 1 hour. (The cold water will keep the potatoes from oxidizing and turning brown.)

2. After 1 hour, remove the potato strips from the bowl and dry them with paper towels. Fill a large saucepan with 2 inches (5 cm) of oil. When the oil is hot, add the potato strips a few at a time (you may have to fry them in batches). Fry the potatoes until they just start to get some color. Remove them from the pan and let them rest until they've cooled down. Just before you're ready to eat, heat the oil in the pan to about 350°F* (180°C) and cook the fries again, stirring them occasionally, until they turn golden brown. Transfer the fries to a baking sheet lined with paper towels, sprinkle them with salt to taste, and serve.

* If the oil has reached the right temperature it should make a sizzling sound when you add a potato strip to the pan; when the potato is done, it should float up to the surface and stay there for one full minute.

PICKLED TURNIPS

Turnips are well loved in the Middle East. In this recipe, all you have to do is toss one red beet into the pickling liquid with the turnips to give them a beautiful pink color. If you like a little more heat, slice the chili or add a second whole chili to the mix.

» **Makes about 2 quarts (2 l)**

2¼ pounds (1 kg) turnips

1 red beet

6 garlic cloves

3 bay leaves

1 whole fresh chili such as jalapeño, serrano, or Fresno

juice from ½ lemon

1 quart (1 l) water

½ cup (1 dl) kosher salt

½ cup (1 dl) distilled vinegar

— *YOU'LL NEED:*
1 jar, about 2 quarts (2 l)

1. Rinse and peel the turnips and the beet, removing the tops. Cut them into 2–3-inch (5–7-cm) pieces and place them in a large clean jar (about 2 qt / 2 l). Add the garlic cloves, bay leaves, chili, and lemon juice. Make sure the jar has a tight-fitting lid. Set it aside.

2. Bring the water to a boil with the salt until the salt has completely dissolved. Pour the boiling water and vinegar over the vegetables, leaving about 1 inch (2–3 cm) of room at the top of the jar. Wipe the rim and seal the jar with the lid, making sure it fits tightly. After the jar has cooled, keep it in the refrigerator for at least one week before using the pickled turnips. They'll last for three or more months in the fridge.

QUICK PICKLED RED CABBAGE

This dish is a quickly made riff on sauerkraut. The salt softens the cabbage and reduces the water content.

» **Makes about 1 quart (1 l)**

1 head red cabbage (about 4½ pounds / 2 kg)

about ¼ cup (½ dl) kosher salt

½ cup (1 dl) distilled vinegar

1. Rinse the cabbage, slice it thinly, and place it in a large bowl. Massage the cabbage with the salt and let it rest for about 20 minutes.

2. After 20 minutes, squeeze the water out of the cabbage with your hands and place it in a clean bowl. Thoroughly rinse the cabbage in water to make sure it isn't too salty.

3. Pour the vinegar over the cabbage, cover the bowl securely, and let it sit on the counter for 3–4 hours (the longer it sits, the better it will be). After several hours, stir the mixture and place it in the refrigerator. Chill for at least 1 hour before eating.

The thing that almost broke me, when we first opened Falafelbaren, our restaurant in Stockholm, was the red cabbage. My uncle's recipe involves massaging salt into shredded red cabbage until it begins to soften. This method was okay as long as I was making 2 pounds (1 kilo) a day, but when we started making up to 25 pounds (12 kilos) a day at the restaurant, my hands got so tired that I began to dread going to work. It took almost a year before I realized that you can simply let the salt work on its own instead.

Börek

"Börek is from Bosnia." "No, Turkey." "No, Greece." "It's called *burek*, not *börek*!"
"No, it's called *burekas*."

It's called börek!

Though it is heavily debated, the consensus seems to be that börek originated
in Turkey. No matter what you call it or where it comes from, it is basically a savory
pie made with phyllo dough.

BÖREK WITH FETA AND SPINACH

» **Makes 4–6 servings**

1 yellow onion

olive oil for frying and
    brushing

feta cheese, about 5 ounces
    (150 g)

about 7 ounces (200 g)
    fresh leaf spinach or
    frozen thawed chopped
    spinach (drain well if
    using frozen)

1 tablespoon sumac

1 package phyllo dough,
    about 20 pastry sheets

sesame seeds

1. Preheat the oven to 400°F (200°C).

2. Peel and chop the onion. Place enough oil to cover the bottom of a frying pan and lightly sauté the onion over low heat. Once the onion is soft, remove the pan from the heat, and allow the onion to cool.

3. In a bowl, crumble the feta cheese (the easiest way is to break it up with your hands) and mix it with the spinach. Add the onions and sumac to the spinach mixture and stir well.

4. Open the package of phyllo dough and unroll the sheets (if you're using frozen phyllo, let it defrost first). Use one sheet at a time if you want more filling than pie, and use more sheets if you like more pie than filling.

5. Place 4–5 tablespoons of the filling in the middle of a phyllo sheet, then roll the phyllo into a long cylinder. Tuck in one end and continue to roll the dough into a coil. Repeat until you've used all of the filling.

6. Put the coils on a baking tray, brush them with oil, and sprinkle with sesame seeds. Bake the pies in the oven for 20–30 minutes, until they've turned a light golden brown.

BÖREK WITH POTATOES

» **Makes 4–6 servings**

1 yellow onion

olive oil for frying and brushing

4 potatoes, peeled and boiled

1 tablespoon dried thyme

1 teaspoon dried lovage

1 teaspoon salt

1 package phyllo dough, about 20 pastry sheets

sesame seeds

1. Preheat the oven to 400°F (200°C).

2. Peel and chop the onion. Place enough oil to cover the bottom of a frying pan and lightly sauté the onion over low heat.

3. To make the filling, mash the potatoes with the onion, thyme, and lovage. Season the mixture with salt and set it aside.

4. Open the package of phyllo dough and unroll the sheets (if you're using frozen phyllo, let it defrost first). Use one sheet at a time if you want more filling than pie, and use more sheets if you like more pie than filling.

5. Place 4–5 tablespoons of the filling in the middle of a phyllo sheet, then roll the phyllo into a long cylinder. Tuck in one end and continue to roll the dough into a coil. Repeat until you've used all of the filling.

6. Put the coils on a baking tray, brush them with oil, and sprinkle with sesame seeds. Bake the pies in the oven for 20–30 minutes, until they've turned a light golden brown.

MEAT
AND FISH

SHAWARMA

Shawarma is the Turkish word for "something that turns or spins"—a reference to the vertical rotisserie on which thin slices of meat are arranged in a cone-like shape. In this recipe, the meat is thinly sliced and then fried in a pan over high heat. Traditionally, lamb (neck or breast) is used to make shawarma, but beef (brisket or chuck) or chicken (boneless thighs) work just as well. Since the slices are cut quite thin and fried over high heat, choose fatty, rather than lean, cuts of meat to cook—it will keep the shawarma tender.

— *FOR THE SHAWARMA*

2¼ pounds (1 kg / about 1
   small head) cauliflower

olive oil for frying

2 eggplants

salt

1⅓ pounds (600 g) lamb
   (neck or breast) or beef
   (brisket or chuck) or
   chicken (boneless thighs)

1 tablespoon shawarma
   spice, see recipe below

— *FOR THE SHAWARMA SPICE*

2 teaspoons sea buckthorn
   powder or curry powder

1 teaspoon dried ginger

1 teaspoon ground black
   pepper

1 teaspoon ground cardamom

1 teaspoon ground cinnamon

2 teaspoons paprika

1 teaspoon garlic powder

2 teaspoons ground cumin

1 teaspoon ground coriander

— *FOR SERVING*

Lebanese pita bread

hummus, see recipe on
   page 84

amba, see recipe on page 55

Jerusalem salad, see recipe
   on page 103

1. Break the cauliflower into small florets with your fingers. Pour a generous amount of oil into a frying pan and sauté the florets for 5–7 minutes, until they have browned. Drain the florets on paper towels and set them aside. Reserve the oil in the pan.

2. Cut the eggplant into quarters about ⅓ inch (1 cm) thick. Salt the eggplant quarters and let them rest in a colander over a bowl for a few minutes to draw out some of the water. Use paper towels to blot off any remaining moisture before placing the eggplant in the pan with the reserved oil. Fry the eggplant over medium-high heat for 7–10 minutes, until it is completely soft. Let the eggplant drain on paper towels and set it aside.

3. Cut the meat into thin strips. In a small bowl, combine all the ingredients for the spice mixture. Place 1 tablespoon of the spice mixture into a large bowl. Add the meat to the bowl and toss it with the spice mix to coat the strips evenly.

4. Pour some olive oil into a large frying pan and cook the meat over high heat for just a few minutes. It won't take long to cook because the slices are so thin.

5. Serve the vegetables and meat with pita bread and bowls of hummus, amba, and Jerusalem salad.

MUSAKHAN

The first time my mom met my dad's family, my grandmother asked if she would like to have some musakhan the next day. My mother, who is Finnish, didn't know exactly what musakhan is, other than a dish made with chicken, and said yes. In the morning, she woke up to the sound of squawking. She looked through the window and saw a dozen chickens running around the yard. She also saw my grandfather, knife in hand, which he was using to slaughter the chickens, one by one, while my grandmother sat next to him, plucking the feathers.

» **Makes 4 servings**

4 large yellow onions

olive oil for frying

½ cup (1 dl) sumac + a little more for garnish

1 teaspoon ground cardamom

salt

freshly ground black pepper

1 whole chicken, about 2¼ pounds (1 kg), cut into pieces, or the equivalent amount of chicken thighs

1 quart (1 l) of water

mana'ish bread, see recipes on page 39, or any other flatbread you like

optional: **roasted pine nuts**

1. Preheat the oven to 350°F (180°C).

2. Peel and dice the onions into ⅓-inch (1-cm) pieces. Pour a generous amount of oil into a large, heavy-bottomed frying pan and sauté the onions over medium heat, stirring occasionally, until the onions have caramelized.

3. Using a slotted spoon, remove the onions from the pan and place them in a bowl. Set the pan aside, reserving the oil.

4. Add the sumac, cardamom, salt, and pepper to the onions in the bowl and stir to combine.

5. Fry the chicken in the pan with the reserved oil over medium heat for about 15 minutes or so (7–8 minutes on each side), turning the chicken at regular intervals so that it browns evenly. Once the chicken has browned, add the water to the frying pan and cook for 15 minutes or so, uncovered, until most of the water cooks off.

6. Add the onion mixture to the chicken. Then remove the pan from the heat.

7. Brush the flatbread with olive oil and top it with the onion mixture and chicken. Place the musakhan in the oven for about 10 minutes to warm through. Remove it from the oven and let it cool down a little. Sprinkle the musakhan with more sumac and roasted pine nuts, if desired, and serve.

CHICKEN AND SPINACH STEW WITH RICE AND PINE NUTS

Spinach is called *sabanekh* in Arabic, and this stew is one of my favorite dishes. My grandmother would always make it for me.

» **Makes 4 servings**

— *FOR THE CHICKEN AND SPINACH STEW*

2 yellow onions

7 garlic cloves

olive oil for frying

1 whole chicken, about 2¼ pounds (1 kg), cut into pieces, or the corresponding amount of boneless thighs

water

1 teaspoon salt

7 ounces (200 g) fresh spinach

— *FOR THE RICE AND PINE NUTS*

about 1½ ounces (40 g) pine nuts

1⅔ cups (4 dl) basmati rice

1 tablespoon butter

1. Peel and chop the onions and garlic.

2. Pour some oil into a deep pan and sauté the onions until they've softened. Use a slotted spoon to remove the onions from the pan and set them aside. Add more oil to the pan and brown the chicken, about 15 minutes. Add enough water to the pan to cover the chicken, then return the onions and garlic to the pan and bring the water to a boil. Lower the heat and let the mixture simmer. Use a spoon or handheld strainer to remove any foam or scum that rises to the top of the water. Add the salt and cook the mixture until the chicken is done, about 20 minutes. Turn the heat off.

3. In the meantime, roast the pine nuts in a dry pan until golden. Remove the pan from the heat and set it aside.

4. Rinse the rice, place it in a strainer and allow it to drain thoroughly. Melt the butter in a saucepan, add the rice, and cook it for a few minutes over medium heat, until all the butter has been absorbed. Stir the pine nuts into the rice and add water according to the directions on the rice package. When the water starts to boil, turn the

heat down to the lowest setting, cover the pan, and cook the rice for about 10 minutes.

5. Add the spinach to the pan with the chicken mixture and cook over medium heat until the spinach softens, about 5–10 minutes. Add a little more water, if needed. Season the chicken and spinach stew with salt to taste and serve it with the rice.

BAKED CHICKEN WITH POTATOES

My grandmother often made this dish for us. It is an all-in-one-pan chicken dinner that is easy to make for the whole family.

» **Makes 4 servings**

2 medium yellow onions

olive oil

juice of 1 lemon

3 tablespoons sumac

½ cup (1 dl) red bell pepper or tomato paste

8 chicken thighs, about 2¼ pounds (1 kg)

18 ounces (500 g) potatoes, such as Yukon Gold or red skin (new potatoes)

3 tomatoes, chopped into quarters

salt

freshly ground black pepper

parsley for garnish

1. Preheat the oven to 350°F (180°C).

2. Peel and chop the onions and fry them in a saucepan with plenty of oil until the onions are soft and transparent. Remove the pan from the heat. Pour the lemon juice and sumac over the onions and add the pepper paste. Mix to combine. Rub the mixture over the chicken and let it marinate for a few minutes.

3. Meantime, slice the potatoes into ½-inch-thick (1.25-cm) slices and boil them for 10 minutes until they're soft. Drain the potatoes and set them aside.

4. Oil a rimmed baking tray and spread the potatoes and tomatoes over the tray. Season with salt and pepper.

5. Place the marinated chicken on top of the potatoes and tomatoes and cover the tray with aluminum foil. Bake the chicken for about 45 minutes. Remove the foil and continue to bake the chicken until it turns golden brown. To test the chicken for doneness, make a small incision in the thigh. If the juices run clear, the chicken is done. Top with chopped parsley and serve.

MOLOKHIA AND CHICKEN STEW

It is traditional to make this popular Egyptian dish with rabbit, but in Palestine it's more common to use chicken. The stew is named after molokhia, a leafy green vegetable that is also known as Jew's mallow (the Latin name is *Corchorus olitorius*). When you cook it, the leaves become gelatinous; in fact, the dried leaves are used to thicken soups. The taste is reminiscent of spinach, and although you might be tempted to use spinach as a substitute, it's best to use molokhia, if you can find it, as the gelatinous quality of the greens really makes the dish. You can sometimes find molokhia at farmers' markets, but your best bet is to look for it in the frozen-foods section of a well-sourced Middle Eastern or Asian grocery store.

» **Makes 4 servings**

— *FOR THE STEW*

½ **yellow onion**

olive oil for frying

1 whole chicken, about 2¼ pounds (1 kg) cut into pieces

1 quart (1 l) of water

1 teaspoon salt

7–10 garlic cloves

1 package (14 ounces / 400 g) frozen chopped molokhia leaves, thawed

— *FOR SERVING*

vermicelli rice, see recipe on page 74

pita bread, see recipe on page 33

lemon slices

1. Peel and chop the onion into ⅓-inch (¾-cm) pieces. Place the oil in a frying pan over medium heat. Sauté the onion in the pan and then set it aside.

2. In a separate pan, fry the chicken over medium heat for about 15 minutes. Make sure there's enough space between the chicken pieces—and turn them over—so that they cook evenly.

3. When the chicken is browned, add it to the pan with the sautéed onion. Add the water and salt to the mixture and cook for 15 minutes over medium heat, without bringing it to a boil.

4. Peel and lightly crush the garlic cloves with a mortar and pestle, a garlic press, or a knife blade. Place some olive oil in a frying pan and sauté the garlic. Once the garlic has softened, pour it and the oil into the pan with the chicken and onion. Add the molokhia to the pan and cook for 5 minutes. Season the stew with salt and remove the pan from heat.

5. Serve the stew with vermicelli rice, pita bread, and lemon slices.

SCHNITZEL

Schnitzel came to Israel with German Jews and has become one of Israel's most popular dishes with both Israelis and Arabs. Traditionally, it's made with veal, which isn't readily available in the Holy Land, so there it's made with chicken or turkey instead—and to make it kosher, oil is substituted for butter. My uncle Khader loves schnitzel and eats it once a week. This is his recipe.

2¼ pounds (1 kg) chicken
or turkey cutlets

— *FOR THE MARINADE*
1 garlic clove, peeled

juice of 1 lemon

1 teaspoon paprika

1 teaspoon ground black
pepper

1 teaspoon salt

1 tablespoon olive oil

— *FOR THE BREADING*
2 eggs

½ cup (1 dl) cornflakes

⅔ cup (2 dl) wheat flour

½ cup (1 dl) breadcrumbs

1 teaspoon salt

1 teaspoon ground black
pepper

oil for frying

— *FOR SERVING*
Jerusalem Salad, see
recipe on page 103

fried potatoes, see recipe
on page 110

taratour, see recipe on
page 48

lemon slices

1. Rinse the chicken cutlets and cut them into thin slices.

2. Mince the garlic and place it in a large bowl. Add the lemon juice, paprika, pepper, salt, and oil. Place the chicken or turkey in the bowl with the marinade, making sure that all the pieces are evenly coated.

3. Marinate the chicken or turkey for at least 1 hour at room temperature or in the refrigerator overnight.

4. Crack the eggs into a bowl and beat them. Crush the cornflakes in a separate bowl and mix in the flour, breadcrumbs, salt, and pepper.

5. Once the meat is marinated, bread the filets. First dip the filets into the beaten eggs and then into the cornflake mixture. Repeat 2 times.

6. Fill a deep straight-sided sauté pan with 2 inches (5 cm) of oil and heat to 350°F (180°C). Fry the schnitzel, a few pieces at a time, turning them once, until they're golden, about 3 minutes per side. When the schnitzel is done, remove it from the oil and drain on paper towels.

7. Serve the schnitzel with Jerusalem salad, fried potatoes, taratour, and lemon slices.

KEBAB

Kebab is a general name for a variety of meat dishes from many different countries, where meat, usually lamb or beef, is cubed, marinated, and grilled on a skewer. The spices and choice of meat vary depending on the country in which it's eaten. In this recipe, the meat is ground, formed into croquettes, and pan-fried (it can be grilled as well). Either way, this is an easy and delicious dish to make.

» **Makes 4 servings**

— *FOR THE KEBAB*

1 onion

1 bunch parsley

2¼ pounds (1 kg) ground
   lamb or beef

1 tablespoon baharat, see
   recipe on page 26

oil for frying

3 or 4 scallions

1 lemon

salt

— *FOR THE SIDES*

pita bread, see recipe on
   page 33

4 lemon wedges or half of
   a lemon, grilled

fried eggplant, see steps
   2–5 on page 99

fried cauliflower, see steps
   2–5 on page 99

quick pickled red cabbage,
   see recipe on page 112

amba, see recipe on
   page 55

skhug, see recipe on
   page 53

pine nuts

taratour, see recipe on
   page 48

1. Finely chop the onion and parsley, preferably in a
   food processor.

2. Mix the chopped onion and parsley in a bowl with
   the meat and baharat. Form the mixture into small
   croquettes and place them on a plate. Cover and
   refrigerate for 30 minutes.

3. Place some oil in a saucepan and sauté the scallions.
   Set them aside.

4. After the meat has marinated, remove it from the
   refrigerator. Add oil to the saucepan and fry the
   croquettes (extra oil may not be needed if the meat
   is fatty). When the croquettes are done, remove
   them from the pan.

5. Squeeze the lemon over the croquettes, salt to taste,
   and serve with your choice of sides.

DOLMAS WITH LAMB AND POTATOES

Like so many dishes that are regularly made in Jerusalem's kitchens, there are several different names for dolmas, which are, quite simply, grape leaves stuffed with rice and meat. If you can't find grape leaves, you can use slightly larger Swiss chard leaves. This recipe contains meat, but it works just as well without it and can be served both hot and cold.

» **Makes 4 servings**

— *FOR THE FILLING*

1 yellow onion

1 scallion

1¼ cups (3 dl) short-grain
    risotto-type rice,
    uncooked

7 ounces (200 g) ground
    lamb or beef

3 garlic cloves

1 tablespoon chopped
    fresh mint

1 teaspoon ground cumin

1 teaspoon ground
    coriander

a pinch of ground
    cinnamon

1 teaspoon salt

a pinch of freshly ground
    black pepper

1 15–16-ounce (450 g) jar
    grape leaves, drained

1. *To make the filling:* Peel and chop the onion and scallion. Soak and rinse the rice thoroughly. In a large bowl, mix together the rice, ground meat, onion, and scallion. Mince or press the garlic cloves and add them to the meat mixture. Add the mint, cumin, coriander, cinnamon, salt, and pepper to the bowl and combine.

2. *To assemble the dolmas:* Remove the grape leaves from the jar or can and unfold them one at a time on a cutting board. Add about 1 teaspoon of filling per grape leaf. Fold the stem end of the leaf over the filling, then fold both sides toward the middle and roll up to the top of the leaf to form a cigar shape. Don't pack the leaves too tightly because the rice will expand when it is fully cooked. Set the stuffed dolmas aside.

3. *To cook:* Peel and slice the potatoes. Heat some oil in a deep saucepan or pot, add the lamb cutlets, and brown them. Add the sliced potatoes along with the chili pepper. Remove the pan from the heat and place the dolmas on top of the potatoes. Pack them tightly. Pour in the tomatoes, water, salt, and pepper. Place a plate on the dolmas to weigh them down so they don't move while cooking. Place the pan back on the stove, with the cover on, and

4 small potatoes

olive oil

2 lamb cutlets, about
3½ ounces (100 g)

1 whole fresh chili pepper

1 can, about 14 ounces
(400 g), whole tomatoes

⅔ cup (2 dl) water

salt

ground black pepper

optional: tomato, sliced, for
garnish

simmer the dolmas over low heat for about 1 hour, until most of the liquid is absorbed.

4. After about 1 hour, remove a dolma from the pan and check to see if the rice is thoroughly cooked. (The time varies depending on the rice you use.) Remove the pan from the heat, uncover, and let the dolmas cool in the remaining liquid for about 20 minutes. To serve, use a slotted spoon to gently transfer the dolmas to a serving dish. Garnish with a few slices of fresh, bright tomato, if you like.

MOROCCAN CHICKEN WITH COUSCOUS

People don't often marry outside of one's religion, but it happens. In my family, my father's uncle married a Jewish woman in the 1960s. Their children were given both Arabic and Hebrew names. The eldest of them is Saleh in Arabic or Schmuel in Hebrew. He married Shoshana, or Shosh as her family calls her. She is originally from Morocco. In the 1950s, about three hundred thousand Jews immigrated to Israel from Morocco, and their food traditions are still a vital part of their lives. While I was writing this cookbook, I asked Shosh to make a typical Moroccan dish, and she came up with this delicious recipe for chicken and couscous. You need two pots and a steamer basket to make this dish. If you don't have a steamer insert, you can prepare the couscous separately.

» **Makes 4 servings**

— *FOR THE CHICKEN*

1 whole chicken, about
  2¼ pounds (1 kg)

water

1 yellow onion

1 quart (1 l) dried
  chickpeas, soaked
  overnight or for at
  least 8–9 hours (not
  from a can)

1 tablespoon turmeric

1 bay leaf

1 teaspoon ground black
  pepper

a pinch of ground cinnamon

— *FOR THE VEGETABLES*

2 carrots

4 potatoes

1 butternut squash

¼ green cabbage

1. Clean the chicken under cold water.

2. Place the chicken in a large pot and cover it with water. Allow the water to come to a boil and then lower the temperature. Use a large spoon or a small handheld strainer to skim off any foam or scum that forms on the surface of the water.

3. Peel and chop the onion. Add the onion, chickpeas, turmeric, bay leaf, pepper, and cinnamon. Let the pot simmer for about 1 hour over low heat.

4. Peel and chop the carrots, potatoes, squash, cabbage, bell pepper, and zucchini into large pieces and place them in a separate large pot. Cover the vegetables with water and add salt. Bring the water to a boil. Once the water is boiling, lower the heat and simmer until the vegetables are tender but still have a little firmness. You can add other vegetables if you like.

5. Place the steamer basket above the stewing vegetables and fill it with the couscous. The steam from the simmering water will cook the couscous. If you don't have a steamer insert, place the

1 bell pepper, any color

1 zucchini

water

salt

— *FOR SERVING*

1¾ cups (4 dl) couscous

hummus, see recipe on
    page 84

olives

couscous in a bowl and pour 1¾ cups (4 dl) of hot water over it. Cover the bowl and let it rest until the couscous has absorbed all of the water

6. After the chicken has cooked for about 1 hour, cut it into pieces. Spoon the couscous onto a large serving platter and place the pieces of chicken on top. Ladle a little chicken broth and some of the chickpeas over the chicken. Add some of the cooked vegetables to the platter as well.

7. Enjoy the meal with hummus and olives.

Fishing has always been important along the coast. The fishermen set out at night and come back early in the morning to sell the fish they've caught at the local market. The smell of fresh fish even has its own word, *zafar*.

From my uncle Samir's terrace, in the fishing port of Akko, you can see fishermen come in with their catch in the mornings. Here, Samir holds a platter of fresh, fried zara, a special fish that is caught only in the spring, when it swims closer to the shore from deeper waters.

FRIED FISH

One of the best ways to enjoy fish is to get it fresh from the sea and fry it quickly. With the leftovers, you can make sayadieh the following day (see recipe on page 142).

» **Makes 4 servings**

2 fresh red chili peppers

7 garlic cloves

olive oil for frying

4 small whole
    Mediterranean fish, e.g.
    sea bass or sea bream

flour

— *FOR SERVING*

fattoush, see recipe on
    page 80

tabbouli, see recipe on
    page 92

taratour, see recipe on page
    48

lemon wedges

1. Chop the chili peppers and garlic. Place a generous amount of oil in a saucepan and quickly sauté the peppers and garlic over fairly high heat, until the garlic is golden brown and the peppers have softened. Set aside.

2. Fill a deep saucepan or deep fryer with about 3 inches (8 cm) of oil and heat it to 350°F (180°C). Lightly bread the fish* in a little flour. Fry the fish until they're golden brown. Remove them with a handheld sieve and drain them on paper towels.

3. Pour the chili pepper and garlic mixture over the fish and serve it with fattoush, tabbouli, taratour, and lemon wedges to squeeze over the fish.

---

* Slice the fish into small pieces if you can't find a saucepan that is big enough to fry them whole.

SAYADIEH

This is a very traditional dish in Akko. *Sayadieh* means "fisherman," and this recipe comes from my uncle Samir's wife, Wafá. The dish is usually prepared with fish that was cooked the day before.

» Makes 4 servings

1¼ cups (3 dl) basmati rice

3 yellow onions

olive oil for frying

1 pound (.45 kg / 4 filets)
    any large white fish

1¼ cups (3 dl) water

a pinch of saffron

1 teaspoon turmeric

1 teaspoon salt

— FOR SERVING

tabbouli, see recipe on
    page 92

taratour, see recipe on
    page 48

1. Rinse the rice and drain it well.

2. Peel and chop the onions. Place some oil in a pan and fry the onion.

3. Cut the fish into cubes and fry it with the onion for 5 minutes.

4. Pour the rice into the pan and add the water, spices, and salt. Bring the water to a boil and let the mixture simmer, covered, over low heat for about 10 minutes. When the rice is cooked, remove the pan from the heat. Serve the sayadieh with tabbouli and taratour.

Tabbouli,
see recipe on page 92

Sayadieh

Taratour,
see recipe on page 48

SWEETS
AND DRINKS

Near the Al-Jazzar mosque in Akko you can buy tradional sweets with almonds, cashews, and sesame seeds sweetened with honey and sugar. You can also buy not-so-tradional pink sweets with cream.

BAKLAVA

Baklava is enjoyed throughout the Middle East—as well as in every country that once belonged to the Ottoman Empire. There are many recipes for the popular pastry, most of which are intensely sweet. My take on baklava is less sweet than most, but I think it tastes better that way.

» **Makes 10–12 servings**

— *FOR THE BAKLAVA*

½ cup (1 dl) whole sweet almonds

½ cup (1 dl) cashews

½ cup (1 dl) pistachios

7 ounces (200 g) ghee (or butter)

1 package (16 ounces) phyllo dough

— *FOR THE SUGAR SYRUP*

⅔ cup (2 dl) granulated sugar

½ cup (1 dl) water

½ cup (1 dl) honey

1 teaspoon freshly squeezed lemon juice

1 teaspoon ground cardamom

1. Preheat the oven to 350°F (180°C).

2. Chop the almonds, cashews, and pistachios. Reserve half of the chopped pistachios for garnish. Place the remaining chopped nuts in a bowl and set aside.

3. Melt the ghee in a double boiler. Prepare a baking pan for the phyllo dough. Preferably choose a pan that is slightly smaller than the phyllo sheets. Grease the pan with ghee. Add a sheet of phyllo and brush it with ghee. Repeat with just under half of the remaining phyllo sheets. Then sprinkle with the nut mixture and continue to layer the rest of the phyllo sheets, brushing them with ghee, until you've used all of the ingredients.

4. With a sharp knife, make a cut from one side of the pan to the other, creating a crisscross pattern with the knife to make diamond-shaped pieces (or square if you like).

5. Put the pan in the oven and bake for about 30 minutes, until the pastry is golden brown and crisp.

6. Meanwhile, prepare the sugar syrup. Heat the sugar and water in a saucepan and stir until the sugar has melted. Stir in the honey. Once the honey is combined with the sugar mixture, remove the pan from the heat and add the lemon juice and cardamom.

7. After 30 minutes, remove the pan from the oven and pour the sugar syrup over the pastry. Sprinkle the reserved chopped pistachios over the top. Let the baklava rest for a bit to give the sugar syrup plenty of time to soak into the pastry.

WATERMELON WITH LABNEH AND ZA'ATAR

My fondest memory of labneh is from Sasa, an area in Galilee. It's located a stone's throw from the Lebanese border. The landscape is similar to Tuscany, with its green, hilly mountains and pleasant climate, even in the middle of summer. In the evenings, we put on thick sweaters to stay warm. The best labneh you can imagine—especially when it is topped with za'atar and lots of olive oil—is made by a man named Kobi, who fled Tel Aviv's hectic life to settle on top of a mountain in Sasa with his herd of hundreds of goats.

Labneh means "yogurt" in most Arabic dialects, except in Egypt, where it means "milk." In this book, it refers to yogurt. If you can't find labneh, use fresh goat-milk yogurt, otherwise any type of regular, all-natural yogurt will work.

» **Makes 4 servings**

1 watermelon (7 ounces (200 g)/person)

1¾ cups (4 dl) labneh, see recipe on page 40

1 tablespoon za'atar, see recipe on page 29

1 tablespoon olive oil

1. Slice the melon and cut it into bite-size pieces. Place the melon in a serving bowl.

2. In a separate bowl, prepare the labneh. Top the labneh with the za'atar and olive oil.

3. Use a fork to dip the melon in the labneh and enjoy.

KNAFEH

Knafeh is originally from the city of Nablus, which is located about 40 miles (65 km) north of Jerusalem. It is a very filling dessert that is made, traditionally, with a local cheese called nabulsi.

» **Makes 8 servings**

— *FOR THE SUGAR SYRUP*

⅔ cup (2 dl) water

⅔ (2 dl) granulated sugar

¼ cup (½ dl) freshly
    squeezed lemon juice

— *FOR THE KNAFEH*

3½ ounces (100 g) nabulsi
    cheese (or fior di latte
    or a similar mozzarella
    that doesn't contain too
    much liquid)

3½ ounces (100 g)
    shredded phyllo dough
    (such as Kataifi)

4 tablespoons (50 g) room
    temperature butter

1. Preheat the oven to 375°F (190°C).

2. To prepare the sugar syrup, combine the water and sugar in a saucepan. Bring the mixture to a boil and stir until the sugar has dissolved. Remove the pan from the heat and add the lemon juice. Stir to combine and set aside to cool.

3. Cut the cheese into small pieces. If you are using regular mozzarella, let it drain for about 1 hour beforehand.

4. Cut the phyllo dough into ⅛-inch-long (½-cm) pieces and put them in a bowl. Add the butter and knead the mixture into a smooth dough.

5. Grease a cast iron skillet and press half of the shredded phyllo dough evenly in the bottom of the pan. Spread the cheese over the dough and then cover it with the remaining phyllo. Press it down firmly. Place the pan over low heat and cook until the bottom of the knafeh is golden brown (the easiest way to check is to gently lift up the phyllo with a spatula).

6. Put the pan in the oven and bake until the phyllo and cheese are golden brown, about 15 minutes. Remove the pan from the oven and let it cool.

7. When the pan is cool, invert it over a dish so that the fried underside of the knafeh is on top. Pour the sugar syrup over the knafeh and let it soak in before serving this rich treat.

DATE BALLS WITH LICORICE

There are many kinds of dates and they—as well as date palms—play an important role in Middle Eastern cultural history. The Prophet Muhammad always ate dates and yogurt for breakfast. Date palm fronds were used on Palm Sunday to greet Jesus as he rode into Jerusalem, and to this day the fronds are also used to celebrate the Jewish holiday of Sukkot.

Although dates contain a lot of sugar, they also boast tons of nutrients and can be served many ways: you can remove the pit and replace it with a candied almond, dip it in chocolate, or make date balls, as in this recipe, which calls for medjool dates. You can use other dates as well, but the consistency may be different, depending on the type you use.

» **Makes 20 balls**

½ **cup (1 dl) pumpkin seeds**

25 **fresh dates, preferably Medjool**

1 **tablespoon cold coconut oil**

3 **teaspoons licorice powder**

2 **tablespoons cocoa**

a pinch of salt

½ **cup (1 dl) flaked coconut or chopped pistachios**

1. Toast the pumpkin seeds. After they've cooled, chop them roughly.

2. Remove the pits from the dates and discard them. Place the dates in a bowl. Add the oil, licorice powder, cocoa, salt, and pumpkin seeds to the bowl. Using your hands, knead the ingredients together. Refrigerate the dough for about 1 hour, which makes it easier to shape.

3. Remove the dough from the fridge and scoop it out, one tablespoon at a time, to shape balls. To finish, roll the balls in coconut or chopped pistachio nuts.

POMEGRANATE SALAD

Removing pomegranate seeds is easy. I usually cut the pomegranate in half with a sharp knife and hold one of the cut halves, seeds facing down, over a plate while I whack the fruit with the back of a wooden spoon. This method can be messy, however, so you can always use the water method. Simply fill a bowl with cold water. Gently break the pomegranate into quarters and immerse them in the water. Carefully nudge the seeds out of the skin to avoid breaking them. When all the seeds have been released into the water, drain them in a colander.

» **Makes 4 servings**

½ **cup (1 dl) walnuts**

2 **pomegranates**

2 **oranges**

a pinch of ground cinnamon

1. Roast the walnuts in a dry pan and then set them aside.

2. Remove the seeds from the pomegranates, using the method you prefer, and place them in a large bowl.

3. Peel and section the oranges. Add the segments to the bowl and stir them gently with the pomegranate seeds.

4. Add the cinnamon to the fruit mixture and stir gently to combine. Garnish with the roasted walnuts and serve.

HARISI

Semolina flour is used in many dishes throughout the Middle East. Harisi is similar to a sponge cake, but semolina gives it a somewhat coarser consistency. Moist but still a bit grainy, this cake is perfect with a cup of coffee!

» **Makes 12 pieces**

7 tablespoons (100 g) room-temperature butter + extra for greasing the mold

2 cups (5 dl) semolina flour

¾ cup (1¼ dl) granulated sugar

a pinch of salt

¼ teaspoon baking soda

1 teaspoon baking powder

¾ cup (1½ dl) + 2 tablespoons plain yogurt

1 can (about 14 ounces / 400 g) condensed sweetened milk

a handful of blanched almond slivers

1. Preheat the oven to 375°F (190°C). Grease a square 8 × 8-inch (20 × 20-cm) baking pan with butter. Set it aside.

2. In a bowl, stir together the butter, semolina, sugar, and salt.

3. In another bowl, combine the baking soda, baking powder, and ¾ cup (1½ dl) yogurt. Add the butter mixture to the yogurt mixture and combine.

4. Pour the batter into the greased pan and smooth the surface with a spatula. Spread the remaining 2 tablespoons of yogurt over the top of the batter. Bake the cake for 30 minutes or so, until it has turned a nice golden color.

5. Remove the cake from the oven and cut it into squares. Pour the condensed milk over the cake while it is still warm. When the cake has cooled down, sprinkle the almonds over the top.

MOROCCAN DONUTS

If the way to happiness is through the stomach, then these Moroccan donuts, or sfenj, as they are called in Morocco, will take you right there. A cross between a donut and a crispy waffle, this is an absolutely winning dessert!

» Makes about 40 donuts

1 ounce (25 g) fresh yeast

1 tablespoon sugar

1 tablespoon salt

2 cups (5 dl) + 1–2 cups
   (2–5 dl) lukewarm water

2 ¼ pounds (1 kg) of flour
   (about 7 cups / 16 dl)

1–2 quarts (1–2 l) of oil for
   frying

powdered or granulated
   sugar

1. In a bowl, combine the yeast, sugar, and 2 cups (5 dl) of water until the yeast dissolves. Wait 30 minutes to let the yeast bloom. After 30 minutes, add the remaining 1–2 cups (2–5 dl) of water, the salt, and the flour, a little at a time, to form a dough. Once combined, let the dough rise for 30 minutes.

2. Heat the oil to 350°F (180°C) in a deep pot or a pan with high sides.

3. To form the donuts, pull off a piece of dough, about the size of a golf ball, and shape it into a ball. Use your fingers to make a hole in the ball of dough, stretch the hole wide to make a ring, and then place the dough in the hot oil. Fry the donuts in batches.

4. When the donuts have turned golden brown, remove them from the oil and place them on a plate lined with paper towels to drain. Sprinkle donuts with powdered or granulated sugar and enjoy.

MUTABBAQ

Roughly translated, the Arabic word *mutabbaq* means "folded." You can find variations of mutabbaq in many parts of the world, but it is thought to have originated in Yemen, where the dish is called malawah. This recipe for sweet cheese pastry is a simplified version of more traditional recipes and yields a deliciously creamy, tangy, sweet, and flaky dessert all at once.

» **Makes 10–12 servings**

— *FOR THE MUTABBAQ*
about 4 ounces (125 g)
 fresh mozzarella

14 tablespoons (1¾ sticks /
 200 g) melted butter

1 package phyllo dough

— *FOR THE SUGAR SYRUP*
⅔ cup (2 dl) granulated
 sugar

½ cup (1 dl) water

½ cup (1 dl) honey

1 teaspoon freshly
 squeezed lemon juice

1. Preheat the oven to 350°F (180°C).

2. Tear the mozzarella into pieces and let it drain in a colander.

3. Grease a pan (slightly smaller than the size of the phyllo sheets) with butter. Lay a single sheet of phyllo in the pan. Brush it with butter. Repeat until half of the sheets are in the pan.

4. Spread a layer of the cheese on top of the phyllo. Lay the remaining sheets of phyllo in the pan, brushing each one with butter as you go.

5. Use a sharp knife to cut the pastry into roughly 2-inch (5-cm) squares, being careful not to cut the bottom layer of pastry, so that the filling doesn't ooze out while it's baking. Place the pan in the oven and bake for about 30 minutes, until the pastry is golden brown.

6. While the pastry is baking, place the sugar and water in a saucepan over medium heat and stir until the sugar has melted. Add the honey and stir until it is thoroughly combined with the sugar-and-water mixture. Remove the pan from the heat and add the lemon juice.

7. When the pastry is done, remove the pan from the oven and pour the sugar syrup over the top. Give the pastry a few minutes to absorb the syrup and cool a bit before serving.

During one of our searches for old olive trees, my uncle Samir and I visited a family in I'billin, whom, we learned, had really old olive trees. They greeted us as if we had known one another for years and showed us their fields and beautiful olive grove. As we were about to leave, we discovered that they also had a lemon tree full of ripe fruit. Before the family had time to grab a ladder, Samir took things into his own hands and used the wall of the house to pick some lemons from the tree.

LEMONANA

Lemonana is a combination of two words from Arabic and Hebrew. *Lemon* means "lemon" and *nana* means "mint." Together they become *lemonana*—a perfect marriage of flavors: lemon, sugar, and fresh mint. You can drink it served over ice or even as a slushy. Whatever you do, drink it ice-cold.

» **Makes about 5 cups [12 dl]**

⅔ cups (2 dl) granulated
   sugar

⅔ cups (2 dl) + 3½ cups
   (8 dl) water

¾ cup (2 dl) freshly
   squeezed lemon juice
   (about 4 lemons)

1 handful of mint

a few lemon slices

• Mix the sugar with the ⅔ cup (2 dl) of water. Stir the mixture until all the sugar has dissolved. Squeeze the lemons over a pitcher and add the remaining water. Stir in the mint and lemon slices. Add plenty of ice before serving.

MINT TEA

Tea originated in China and spread from there. Today, people drink tea all over the world. In many countries in the Middle East, Chinese gunpowder green tea is served in small, ornate glasses as a welcome drink for both expected and unexpected guests. Traditionally, it's very sweet and usually flavored with fresh mint, although other herbs like verbena, wild oregano, and sage are used as well. Serving mint tea is an art in itself, where the teapot is lifted high above the glass to help aerate and blend the flavors. To make the tea, you'll need a metal teapot.

» **Makes about 4 cups [1 l]**

1 quart (1 l) water

2 teaspoons gunpowder
    green tea

1 bunch mint

optional: granulated sugar
    to taste

1. Boil the water. Pour some hot water into the metal teapot, swirl it around, and then pour it out. This will both clean the pot and keep it warm.

2. Add the tea to the teapot and pour in 1 cup of hot water. Let the tea steep for about one minute and then pour it into a glass. This is referred to as "minding the tea's soul," and in this glass you will find the finest aromas from the tea leaves. Reserve this glass of tea.

3. Pour an additional cup of hot water into the pot. Wait a minute and pour it into a second glass. (You'll notice that the color is different from the first brewing.) Discard this brewing. Pour the tea that was reserved from the first brewing into the teapot, and then add fresh water to the pot until it is three-quarters full.

4. Put the teapot on the stove over medium heat and allow it to gently come to a boil. When the water boils, remove the pot from the heat and add the mint and sugar, if you like. Pour the tea into a glass and then pour it back into the pot. Repeat this two or three times so that the tea mixes properly.

5. Serve the tea in individual glasses. Garnish with additional fresh mint leaves.

ARABIC COFFEE

By volume, coffee is the best-selling commodity in the world. Per capita, Swedes and Finns drink more coffee than anyone, but coffee originally came from the Arabian Peninsula, or more specifically, Yemen. Arabic coffee is sometimes called Turkish coffee because the Ottoman Empire was responsible for spreading it throughout the world.

The most important thing to know about making Arabic coffee is this: the coffee should be ground as fine as possible, even finer than espresso. If you can, buy whole beans that you can grind yourself or have them ground at your local coffee shop.

» **Makes 4 cups (1 l)**

about 2 tablespoons (28 g) finely ground coffee

1¼ cups (3 dl) cold water

optional: **granulated sugar**

optional: **ground cardamom or ground cinnamon**

1. Place the coffee and water in a small, heavy saucepan—or use a special pot, usually made from copper and designed specifically for Arabic coffee—over medium heat, stirring it constantly.

2. When it begins to simmer, remove the pan or pot from the heat. Let it rest for a few moments so the coffee grinds can settle to the bottom.

3. Pour the hot coffee into small cups and serve it with sugar, cardamom, or cinnamon to taste.

The hookah, or nargile, is immensely popular in the Arabic culture. Although very bad for your health it serves as a reason to meet over a cup of coffee and smoke the fruit-flavored tobacco, sometimes for hours.

The lady in sunglasses centrally featured in the café is Umm Kulthum—known as the voice of Egypt and the Arab world's greatest singer. Even today, over forty years after her death, you cannot be awake a day without hearing at least one of her songs.

Cats have a special place in Islam. The Prophet Muhammad loved cats and had a favorite, named Muezza. According to legend, whenever Muezza fell asleep on his prayer clothes, Muhammad would simply cut off a piece of the garment so that the cat could continue to sleep undisturbed. Cats are considered to be clean and may live in both homes and mosques. It is common to see cats wandering around Akko, especially near the Al-Jazzar mosque.

{ ACKNOWLEDGMENTS }

It has been my lifelong dream to write a book. Therefore, it is with great humility that I would like to thank everyone who has helped make this book a reality.

Thank you, Eva Kruk and Bonnier Fakta for giving me the chance. Linnéa Von Zweigbergk for all the help with the text. Lennart Weibull for all the fine pictures. Sara R. Acedo for the design of the Swedish edition of this book. My brother Aadel for coming with me on this journey. My youngest brother, Samir, who helped me in the kitchen. My uncle Samir in Akko, who showed us around the whole city. Thanks to my uncle Saleh and his wife Shosh, who familiarized us with Moroccan culinary traditions. My aunt Husnye, who baked mana'ish and took us out to pick wild herbs. My dad and mom, who introduced me to the kitchen. Thanks to my whole family in Palestine, all of whom contributed to making this book a reality.

And thanks to Jenny, whom I'm lucky to call my wife, because you always go along with my crazy ideas and stop them when they're completely out of control. I hope you understand how grateful I am that you're by my side.

»»»»»

Nidal Kersh is a restaurateur in Stockholm, Sweden, where he is the owner of Falafelbaren, the city's first falafel restaurant. *Jerusalem Food*, Kersh's first book, was originally published in Sweden in 2017 under the title *Shakshuka*.

{ INDEX }

Pages in **bold** refer to main recipe pages.

STERLING EPICURE
New York

An Imprint of Sterling Publishing Co., Inc.
1166 Avenue of the Americas
New York, NY 10036

ISBN 978-1-4549-3292-5

Distributed in Canada by Sterling Publishing Co., Inc.
c/o Canadian Manda Group, 664 Annette Street
Toronto, Ontario M6S 2C8, Canada
Distributed in the United Kingdom by GMC Distribution Services
Castle Place, 166 High Street, Lewes, East Sussex BN7 1XU, England
Distributed in Australia by NewSouth Books
University of New South Wales, Sydney, NSW 2052, Australia

For information about custom editions, special sales, and premium and corporate purchases,
please contact Sterling Special Sales at 800-805-5489 or specialsales@sterlingpublishing.com.

Manufactured in China

2 4 6 8 10 9 7 5 3 1

sterlingpublishing.com

Cover design by Igor Satanovsky
Interior design by Shannon Nicole Plunkett
Cover photography: Elena Eryomenko/Shutterstock.com
Illustrations: Marchenko Oleksandr/Shutterstock.com
Endpapers: Roman Yanushevsky/Shutterstock.com (Front), Russian Kalnitsky/Shutterstock.com (Back)